POSTMODERN PERSPECTIVES ON CONTEMPORARY AMERICAN LITERATURE

POSTMODERN PERSPECTIVES
ON
CONTEMPORARY AMERICAN LITERATURE

Editors

Sanjeev Kumar

Dr Anuradha

AUTHORSPRESS

Worldwide Circulation through Authorspress Global Network
First Published in 2021
by
Authorspress
Q-2A Hauz Khas Enclave, New Delhi-110 016 (India)
Phone: (0) 9818049852
E-mail: authorspressgroup@gmail.com
Website: www.authorspressbooks.com

Postmodern Perspectives on Contemporary American Literature
ISBN 978-93-91314-88-0

Printed in India at Thomson Press (India) Limited

Dedicated to
Our Loving Parents

Acknowledgements

Remembering all those who are associated with the editing of this book is a matter of pleasure and pride. We are grateful to all those who have made our editing work a gratifying and enlightening task. We express our sincere gratitude to reverent scholar Dr. Himanshu Parmar, Associate Professor, Department of English, Himachal Pradesh University, Shimla for his insights and constant propositions throughout the process of editing of this book. We are also thankful to Dr. Ashok Verma, Professor, Dept. of English, Bhagat Phool Singh Mahila Vishwavidyalaya, Khanpur Kalan, Sonipat (Haryana), for his encouragement and continual guidance throughout the process of bringing out this book. We thank Mr. Shubham, Assistant Prof. of English, Govt. P.G. College, Naraingarh (Ambala) for his sittings and discussions on several issues and in analysing various papers included in this anthology. We also thank Dr. Urmil Rawat and Ms. Vasandra for their timely support and encouragement which helped us in numerous ways.

We are indebted to Rajni and Suresh, our family, for the sacrifice of their time and energy which boosted our morale to carry out this task successfully. Our kids – Arindam, Agastya, Pavishka and Daakshit deserve a special place here for it has been their love and affection which kept instilling in us the spirit to finish this task timely and efficiently.

Finally, we are thankful to the publishers and the contributors without whom the book would not have been possible.

Sanjeev Kumar
Anuradha

Preface

The present anthology, *Postmodern Perspectives on Contemporary American Literature*, is a venture to portray and comprehend diverse layers of literary, cultural, historical, socio-political and psychological stratum of American literature in postmodern times. It attempts to map out, in its diversified forms, the inherent critical perspectives of American life and it's Americana in varied ways and means. Such perspectives unearth the vagueness, worthlessness and nothingness of contemporary life which, in one way or the other, deconstructs the set beliefs and norms associated with a literary work in the postmodern society.

A brief investigation of what is America and who is an American, to begin with, would be in place here as it is imperative to know how a nation is shaped and influenced by a great historic past before we talk about contemporary American literature. Continuity and the sense of it made America the oldest independent country of the American continent that boasts of having an old political entity and the oldest written constitution in the world. Since the inception of America as a new entity or nation, the American thought himself as a new man who acts on novel principles and must entertain new ideas and opinions leaving behind involuntary idleness, dependence, helplessness and useless toil and march forward with hope and light and with ample subsistence. This march, however rapid and successful, had an unsettled issue – the American identity or what it means to be an American which has remained a great theme of American literature. Walter Allen maintains:

> Americans, it seems, today as much as at any time, today perhaps more than ever in the past, must always seek to define and evaluate their differences from the other peoples of the world. Are they in fact different, and what has made them so? And, assuming they are different, what have they in common with one another? (6)

American studies got impetus from D. H. Lawrence's *Studies in Classic American Literature* (1923) which proves to be one of the best studies on the subject. All the critical interpretations which follow Lawrence, do not include every aspect of American literature. One can see clashes between the 'genteel' school and 'frontier' school represented by Henry James and Mark Twain respectively. A more serious study, one can say, would centre on 'romance' and 'realism.' On the whole, Ian Ousby argues, earlier critics focused on realist novels that "deal with contemporary issues and with the individual in society" (11). Later critics, Ousby asserts, put emphasis on writers of romance "whose main preoccupation is with man alone or man and nature, rather than man and society" (11). Before we look at postmodern perspectives on contemporary American literature, a historical glimpse of American literature and letters would be in place here to have a better understanding of the trends and issues in American literature since the beginning of twentieth century.

The advent of the twentieth century was not as encouraging for literature as it was for the last decade of the nineteenth century. In 1890s, there were realist, romantics, naturalists, impressionists, symbolists, decadents, socialists and Harvard poets who had talent and conviction and almost everything but not a sympathetic readership that could accept these outspoken and experimental writers. This proved fatal and the writing succumbed before the Genteel Tradition which believed that a good book should be 'decent' that could 'safely' be placed before and read by young girls. The 1910s, however, saw a sunny season after a long literary winter when the writers started breaking tradition and adopted a critical tone for American life and institutions with an essentially patriotic impulse. They focused on subject matter and paid a little attention, except Eliot, Frost and Cather, to the structure and texture of their writings.

The 1920s was another literary spring after the cold rains of WWI and its aftermath. The writers, for instance Faulkner, with almost no regard for tradition, followed European, especially French, ideals of the literary life. There were, nonetheless, writers like Pound and Eliot, Proust and Joyce who served as models and became known as the Lost Generation. Their general emphasis, writes Malcolm Cowley, was on "form rather than subject matter, with the result that they produced better-finished and more complicated works than did most of their immediate predecessors" and their works became "distinguished by intensity and depth rather than by any broad vision of the nation or the world" (xxix). There was yet another little regeneration in the New York ghetto which is popularly known as Harlem Renaissance that is specifically devoted to African Americans' literature. It was a time when Harlem was in vogue and the black Americans produced literature in their African Blues and Jazz and consequently attempted to recoup their identity in a Jim Crow world. Writers like Langston Hughes and Claude

McKay protested against racial discrimination in America and demanded equal footing in the making of America and realising American dream.

During the Great Depression of 1930s, American writers started taking a new cue in writing and liked to be called proletariats or revolutionaries in the beginning of this decade and social realist after 1935. They believed that literature should address the cause of the workers or the proletariat with a focused doctrine – inevitable downfall of capitalism or the crusade against fascism. Writers like Dos Passos and Hemingway produced novels that do not betray the aforesaid doctrine and attack on monopoly capitalism or deal with the anti-fascist crusade. The American literature of 1940s, largely affected by WWII, added nothing more than the knowledge of how soldiers felt and acted. It was a time when war preoccupied all the genres of American literature and added little to it. The postwar years, especially 1950s, saw a sudden rise in criticism and new methods were being applied to interpret and reinterpret the old masterpieces. Critics looked at the works of the twentieth century in relation to what had gone before and, Cowley asserts, demonstrated that American literature was "more consistent and more unified than anyone had suspected in the past" (xxxi).

The American writers, as a matter of fact, saw and wrote about two Americas – the real and the ideal. The first one is the geographic location and the second one is a state of being that answers all human hopes. American literature, an alert reader finds, is centered on the clash between the real and the ideal America and there is a usual reaction or protest from the other if one America finds prominence over the other. This results in, state Stern and Gross, rebelliousness in American literature:

> American literature is a rebellious and iconoclastic body of art. The puritan rebelled against the Anglican, the deist against the Puritan, the romantic against aspects of deism, the naturalist against aspects of romanticism, the symbolist against aspects of naturalism. In each case the rebellion was greeted with cries of outrage and prophecies of doom (ix).

Postmodern American literature is a continuum and yet a break away from offset uniformity, homogeny and selectiveness of modern literature. It is a shift from paradigms established by euro-centrism and its superiority in modern literature. The contemporary American literature emphasises metaphorical presentations of things in a dissimilar way which stands for self-reflexivity, resilience, self-questioning and hybrid styles. One can see in American literature today what Lyotard asserts to be features of postmodernism, that the "postmodern would be that which, in the modern, puts forward the unpresentable in presentation itself; that which denies itself the solace of good forms, the consensus of a taste which would make it possible to share collectively the nostalgia for the attainable" (81).

Contemporary American literature exemplifies various postmodern techniques such as intertextuality, hyperreality, historiographic metafiction, hysterical realism, magical realism and absurdism. The readers can find an elaborate discussion on Postmodernism and American literature in the introductory essay "The Literary Post-Modern and American Literature: An Overview" luminously written by Dr. Himanshu Parmar. The papers included in the book highlight myriad layers of postmodernism in contemporary American literature in diverse ways ranging from Barth's sexual innuendo and its metafictional interpolations to postmodern reading of Vonnegut and to family as metanarrative in Malamud. There is also a glimpse of postmodern aesthetics in contemporary American literature, self-reflexivity in Paul Auster, hyperrealism in David Foster Wallace, the black predicament in Walker and Morrison, postmodern essence in Silko and Momaday to demystification and paradox in Lahiri. The papers, the readers will note, have diverse layers of contemporary American literature and its postmodernity.

The introduction of the book "The Literary Post-Modern and American Literature: An Overview," makes a distinction between the Western and the Oriental thought clusters and emphasises how the Western Literary Canon is steeped in non-literary discourses and which is also followed in postmodernism. Dr. Himanshu Parmar brilliantly explains different strands of postmodernism and argues, in the line of Andreas Huyssen, that the entire construct of postmodernism seems to be falling asunder because of the juxtapositioning of myriad points-of-view. Nonetheless, the postmodern can be taken as the extension of the traditional as well as the modern and the three, i.e. traditional, modern and postmodern, work together creating a chain of thought and interpretation. Dr. Parmer, after a critical view of postmodernism, discusses briefly the history of American literature and maps out myriad strands of contemporary American literature. He asserts that one significant aspect of American postmodernism is the 'new kind of nation building discourse that glorifies the multicultural and multiethnic nature of America.'

The first paper "Sexual Innuendo in John Barth's *Lost in the Funhouse:* Metafictional Interpolations" gives details of a riotous tale of a visit to a funhouse and the discovery by Ambrose of his body and the self. Dr. Harpreet Kaur Vohra tells that the sexual insinuations of the story have received much attention by critics and have been variously interpreted. The tale has been construed on different tangents owing to its highly plastic and unconventional story-telling technique but what cannot be missed are the metafictional techniques employed. The paper examines the sexual innuendos in the story through its metafictional interpolations. Patricia Waugh's interpretation of metafiction is used as the framework to analyse the self-reflexivity of the work. How sex permeates the text and becomes the driving force through metafictional interpolations points to the fact that postmodern interpretations can lend several unusual dimensions to a text and also form the very basis of its language.

The next paper deals with Kurt Vonnegut's novel, *Slaughterhouse Five* also known as *The Children's Crusade: A Duty-Dance with Death*, as a postmodernist piece of work, exhausting all the dimensions for which postmodernism stands. This school associates itself with everything that came after and as an effect of World War II, the onset of consumerism, globalisation and the psychological trauma that came as the side effect. This theory rejects the rigid boundaries and structures thus allowing itself to go absurd and inter-genre. The narrative of the novel, Harsimran and Shubham assert, is explicitly postmodern in its style and combines everything that comes under its patronage, be it metafiction, fabulation, intertextuality, poioumena, irony, play, black humour, pastiche, temporal distortion, paranoia and fragmentation. Kurt Vonnegut combines the autobiographical elements with fiction, being himself the American prisoner of war during World War II. The narrative style which he adopts further deepens the horrors of war and its after effects on war survivors. Postmodernism stands for all, that is incoherent, non-linear, absurd, and alien which the novel successfully depicts through its protagonist, Billy Pilgrim. The novel and the style it adheres to, move away from all that is constructivist, realist and from all other modern approaches. Shubham and Harsimran explore all the postmodern elements used by the author in its writing style. Claimed as a purely metafictional novel by critics, it is more than metafiction alone. The paper explores all the intertextual aspects used, and the ways in which metafiction, irony, fragmentation, and temporal distortion come into play to make *Slaughterhouse Five* a masterpiece of postmodern American fiction.

The third paper by Dr. Anju and Dr. Pooja, "Judaism and American Culture Interface: Family as a Metanarrative in Bernard Malamud's *The Fixer*" explores the views of the Jewish-American novelist regarding the erosion of family ties through postmodernist analysis of his novel *The Fixer*. In the context of interpersonal ties, the novel presents Malamud's radical views regarding Jewish family traditions, the writers maintain. The novelist is not a blind follower or advocate of Jewish religious ideologies or rabbinical prescriptions. Many of the characters in the novel, Dr. Anju and Dr. Pooja argue, can be seen caricaturing and parodying the traditional Talmudic heroes and their kith and kin. In *The Fixer*, Malamud shows not only Americans but also Russian-Jews respectively as discarding the outdated Jewish emphasis on customs and family. He shows the Jews especially the second and the latter generations sceptical of the orthodox Judaic familial metanarratives and unwilling to follow them as they find these ideologies in direct conflict with their success dreams. Malamud's concern with Judaism relates more to its utility than to its religiosity. He shows that the American-Jews keep their personal and family lives separate from religious dogmas. They like to create their homes with whosoever they love irrespective of any race, ethnicity and religion. To take an example from the novel, *The Fixer*, the characters wish to be called themselves as "free thinkers" than 'Jews'.

The fourth paper in this anthology "Post-Modern Aesthetics in Contemporary American Literature: The Philosophy of Existentialism" examines existentialism from a post-modern philosophical perspective. Dr. Maroua Rogti asserts that the philosophy of existentialism and the theory of postmodernism may appear as two different thoughts having multiple directions. The former is a philosophy of human being and the latter is a theory familiarised with social inquiry instead of individual existence. As modern literature has long been considered to be the mirror which tempts to reflect society, postmodern literature became associated with those who strongly believe in aesthetic, artistic, and rhetoric portrayal of individuals in literacy writings. Hence, Dr. Rogti asserts, postmodernism seeks to deal with upheavals in representation, disuse of consistency theories of truth, secular reason, and particular plans of progress derived from the Age of Enlightenment.

Dr. Urmil Rawat's paper "New Dimension to the Dichotomous Worlds in Joanna Russ' *The Female Man*" explores the cultural conflict of gender roles in the text *The Female Man* of Joanna Russ, a feminist science fiction writer. The study focuses on utopian and dystopian state to realise the possibility to confront the patriarchal mindset. The gender will be studied in isolation and in relation to the other, with the thought process going into the praxis of their creation and sustenance by judging their vitality. The emphasis in both the worlds, Dr. Rawat maintains, is on future feminist evolution. Feminist utopia is a place where women are not judged, governed or discriminated on the basis of their gender. It is a world with equal distribution of opportunities, rights and duties. It negates the dictate of the existing culture that women are to assist and sustain men to the point of subservience. Hence it is a visualised state which proves to be a catalyst in cultural conflict. Dystopia on the contrary, is a world in which gender inequalities breed and women are too frail to grapple with the cultural shell to condone it.

The sixth paper "American Railways in the Time of Postmodernism: A Discourse on Contemporary Literature" explores the negligence of the American railways in 1970s by the government in the development and management of railways because of the expenditure cost of railways and long term actions, which was usually unaccepted/rejected by the then political leaders. In the paper, Sudipta Sardar explains how Amtrak was introduced to regain the lost momentum of the railways. American literature, specifically in the decades of 1970s and 1980s presented railways as an attraction, carrier of an age old system, notion of nostalgia, silent travelling and a thing of pastime pleasure. The postmodern literature carries the image of the railways as a utility less degraded system, trying to keep up its lost glory with a nostalgic urge. In the novel *A Farewell to Arms,* Hemingway uses railways metaphorically to represent the hopelessness of the present society as compared to the lost decades of peace and joyfulness. But postmodern literature hints at the reincarnation of the lost glory of railways and would regret losing railways and its energy efficiency and comfortable travel. Thus, American post-modern literature is nostalgic in the postmodern period but translating that nostalgia into support for railways in the 21st century is a challenge, as presented in various literary works of this decades.

Dr. J. Iswarya, in her paper "Self-Reflexivity in the Select Novels of Paul Auster" maintains that the novelist attempts to personify his own character that is torn between the randomness of the massive stretch of his country and the complexity of his inner-self that strains to make sense of its existence. His protagonists are all impatient men on quests who thirst for the impeccable knowledge of their identity, going through inexplicable patterns that often mislead them beyond imagination, bestowing upon them with nothing but the experience of it. This experience and awareness make them lose their innocence and going one step further, lose their identity, taking them farther away from their goal. The postmodern potpourri makes them lose their faces, purpose and even their souls. The multiple selves are created purposefully in the image of the writer's self as he is no longer satisfied with the externalised journey of the physical. He hungers to conduct his 'self' on a journey to a higher 'self' that is primarily psychological and pragmatically spiritual. Hence, Auster, Dr. J Iswarya asserts, chooses 'metafiction' as the mode of journey through space, a journey from the 'self' to reach the 'self.' This paper attempts to establish 'self-reflexivity' as the strategic phenomenon that is observed in most of his works to emphasise the postmodernity in them.

The eighth paper "An Intrinsic Insight into the Contemporary Post-Modern Literary Image of 'Hyperrealism' in the Lens of David Foster Wallace" highlights the perspective and vision of the novelist, who often threw insight into the sarcastic study of American culture in the arena of postmodernist writing. It is an attempt to bring to foreground some of the unexplored aspects of post-postmodern fiction in the physical nature of the literal artifact in reinvigorating the interchange between the reader and the literary text. Dr. Aditi Abhishikta explains that the most persuasive enunciations of his numerous prerogatives are those of 'E Unibus Pluram: Television and U.S. Fiction,' which came in 1993 where Foster Wallace claims for what he intends to tag 'hyperrealism,' 'fiction of the image,' and 'postmodernism,' a denunciation of caustic styles and insolences, which is assumed to be characteristic mark of postmodernist literature, and in view of a change in the course of a 'single-entendre' narrative, one that catches realism by replacing or augmenting the usually infertile instincts of criticism with those of productive ethical commitment and the retrieval of language's referential execution. Although a good number of critics, opponents, reviewers and authors observed on post-postmodernist propensities in the epochs following Foster Wallace's periodical of these urgings, it has taken quite few years for them to add an adhesion, and the reviewers only established on something like an illustrator for them upon periodical, in 2010, of Adam Kelly's 'David Foster Wallace and the New Sincerity in American Fiction.'

In the next paper "Predicament of Black Women: Racism and Abuse in Alice Walker's *The Colour Purple* and Toni Morrison's *The Bluest Eye*," Ms. Anshuman attempts to depict the plight of black women and their subjugation in myriad ways in the American capitalist society. She describes that from the times immemorial women have been subjugated and subjected to atrocities like oppression, discrimination and gender biasness but female subjugation and hostile sexism raises two fold with appearance of the word 'black'. The experience of life for black women is way more harsh and suppressing than the white ones, as the perpetrators in many cases are not only white men and women rather the men of their race too. Millions of narratives worldwide are devoted exclusively for women experience but black female experience has carved a niche for itself in the mainstream contemporary American literature. The novels in question, Anshuman maintains, depict how the black women have been socially, politically and psychologically neglected and subjected to barbarity and brutality in specific inhuman conditions.

Ms. Radhika, in her paper "*Beloved*: A Postmodern Voice to the Unvoiced Slavery" discusses the novel as a combination of historical facts and fiction and portrays postmodern counter narrative that carries a critical meaning and silenced memory of slave community. Toni Morrison, through her novel, tries to give voice to and against the unvoiced slavery system. She combines the past to the present and rediscovers the experiences of the African American slavery which nullified the existence of the black Americans. Morrison, through her characters, travels time that has a psychological impact on the people. Beloved, the ghost, remains silent throughout the novel but her stillness gives the voice to the suppressed.

The next paper "Postmodernism in the Writings of Toni Morrison" is an attempt to deal with political views of the eighteenth and nineteenth centuries with the philosophical notions of the twentieth century. Ms. Upanisha depicts how Morrison employs a stream of consciousness technique in order to retain the flow of thoughts and memories of various characters, and augment the poignancy of their circumstances in her creative works. Morrison weaves a complex narrative not only attempting to counter standards of race and gender but also drawing the focus on nuanced aspects like the woman's freedom to express her sensuality through characters like China, Poland, Miss Marie, Sula, Eva, Hannah, and even Dorcas.

The twelfth paper "Leslie Marmom Silko's *Ceremony* and N. Scott. Momaday's *House Made for Dawn*: Reflection of Post-Modern American Essence" explores psychological transformation of people in contemporary American society. Vijaykumar Ganpatrao Pawar seeks to unveil the realistic situation of the age in the works of Leslie Marmon Silko and N. Scott. Momaday. He further explains that the novels *Ceremony* and *House Made of Dawn* by the respective writers can be taken as the representative works of the age as the writers present the real essence of the age through these works. A sense of negativity that has been overtly observed amongst the individuals is accurately described through the novels. They explore the contemporary evils that were prevalent in the society like: cultural plurality, racial conflict, economic and political supremacy of the dominant cultures at societal level and alienation, depression, psychological antipathy and a sense of nothingness at individual level. The paper analyses the novels in question under the light of representing the conditions of the age as explored by the writers and simultaneously decoding the multiple layers of cultural dislocation and psychological confrontation faced by the individuals in the form of the novel characters.

The next paper "Postmodern Canons and American Literature" deals with various ideas of postmodernism in context with Frederic Jameson, Jean-Francois Lyotard and Jean Baudrillard. Dr. Anum Mirza maintains that postmodernism culture brought new changes in art and philosophy which is a reaction against modernism. The postmodern writers reject the themes, style and the techniques of the modern writers and use the postmodern devices such as pastiche, magic realism, intertextuality, and fragmentation in their works. Jameson deconstructs the Marxian ideology from the perspective of contemporary society and the forces of change and transformation of the West. Jean Francos Lyotard analysed the nature of knowledge and its role in society and explored the meta-narratives. He asserted that the growth of science and technology led to the growth of communication, mass media and computer. Lyotard advocated the multiplicity of society and surreal literary devices to articulate the complex nature of society. Linda Hutcheon explained the postmodernist puzzle and argued that the postmodernism itself is paradoxical in nature. She reiterated that postmodernism is both over-defined and under-defined since it has so many definitions. Frederic Jameson rejected all stylistic techniques including parody and argued that in the postmodern age pastiche is the right and suitable stylistic technique to articulate the contemporary malaise of the American people.

The last paper "Demystifying the Paradox of First and Second Generation Diaspora: An Analytic Study of *The Namesake*" explores film adaptation of Jhumpa Lahri's novel *The Namesake* portraying the paradigm shift in the psyche of the second-generation diaspora. The oscillating motion between the two cultures brings about different set of crises, and the defence mechanism that individuals use to cope with it, also differs. The fact that both, the creator, and re-creator of this fine piece of work are women of Indian origin, living abroad, explains the addition of their personal sensibilities associated with living with twin cultures. Being generation apart, and being brought up in an extremely polarised environments, the lives of the characters of *The Namesake* portray the classic exemplification of difference is values, ethics, moralities, and in the overall way of living. The aim of this study is to highlight the in depth polarities which develop within the individuals who share everything, but not their outlook towards life.

All the aforesaid papers included in this anthology provide varied glimpses of contemporary American life and its Americana. The present book, the editors hope, would cater to the needs of the scholars interested in American literature and its contemporary postmodernity which is as diversified as America itself is. Through a close analysis of some of the more important postmodern perspectives of contemporary American literature, this book, we hope, would create its special place in the mind and heart of its readers. The editors invite all the suggestions/critical views that can improve the quality of the contents of the book in one way or the other.

Sanjeev Kumar
Anuradha

Works Cited

Allen, Walter. *The Urgent West: The American Dream and Modern Man.* E.P. Dutton & Co., Inc., 1969.

Cowley, Malcolm. "Preface". *American Literature Survey: The Twentieth Century*, edited by Milton R. Stern & Seymour L. Gross, Penguin Books, 1977, pp. xxv-xxxi.

Lyotard, Jean Francois. *The Postmodern Condition: A Report on Knowledge.* U of Minnesota P, 1984.

Ousby, Ian. *A Reader's Guide to Fifty American Novels.* Arnold Heinemann, 1979.

Stern, Milton R. & Gross, Seymour L. *American Literature Survey: The Twentieth Century.* Penguin Books, 1977.

Contents

INTRODUCTION

The Literary Post-Modern and American Literature: An Overview

Himanshu Parmar

> With postmodernism it is as if we pass through the looking-glass of western reason.
>
> (Qtd. in Wain, 359)

The disparate lines of thought that intersperse the intellectual storehouse of the world, spatio-temporally, are broadly categorised into two clusters: the Western and the Oriental. While the Western line of thought derives its genesis, as Culler points out, in the Greek and the Hebraic traditions, the Oriental owes itself, saliently, to the Indian and the Persian. Whilst the primary questions that the two strands have explored and negotiated, in literature or philosophy, overlap, their manifestations, and subsequent disseminations, have found disparate paradigms. Talking of literature, both the intellectual lines of thought have primarily focused on the 'nailing' of meaning of a text and negotiating the centrifugal forces therein. Philosophy, an apparently larger paradigm, subsuming literature, too, in its "centripetality", has sought answers to the questions of meaning of life: Where do we come from, where do we go after death and what do we do in-between.

Seeking pardon for the generalisations made above, pertaining to the two "clusters", it is submitted that this was done to highlight a significant quality of the western Literary Canon that is extended as well as compromised by the domains and arches of Postmodernism. This critical feature also marks a decisive distancing between the Western and the Oriental lines of thought: the connection to the tradition. While the Oriental Canon of thought has always prided in its connectedness with what preceded; the Western Canon has 'prided' on its being founded on a "system of replacement", as Leah Wain puts it. In the western canonical tradition, the 'new' systems of thought and theory have emphasised on superseding the existing with an apparent 'better' way of understanding and interpreting.

The Western Literary Canon, in addition to this, in the first half of the 20th century, exorbitantly 'loans' ideas from various non-literary modes of thought. The entire paradigm of Western Literary Theory is steeped in non-literary discourses, focusing on a specialised perspective to look at a text, and, in the wake, extending a lackadaisical approach towards the conventional mode of interpreting literature, teaching with entertainment: what Horace defines in *Ars Poetica*:

> Who can blend usefulness and sweetness wins every Vote, at once delighting and teaching the reader. (178)

Consequently, contemporary analysis and critical understanding of a text has become theory specific: Feminist study, Marxist study, Psychoanalytic study, etc., each approaching a text with consecrated devotion to a non-literary mode of thought, negating any alternative meanings that may be found in it. Meaning, in other words, has been reduced to a set of formulas employed on a text: changing the formula brings out a 'new' textual facade.

Postmodernism, too, at a glance, seems to follow the same beaten track of Western Canon of Thought when it, as West puts it, "attempts a radical break with all of the major strands of Post-Enlightenment thought" (Qtd. in Wain). The term postmodernism made its first forays into literature, as a term, to define fictional writings that were composed after Modernism and were experimental in nature. Given the fact that Modernism as a literary movement was, in itself, an umbrella term that accommodated experimental writings at the dawn of the 20th century, Post-modern "experimentation", logically, had to stand in contradiction to the Modernist Experiment.

The very primary and basic definitions of Modernism and Postmodernism are highly reflective of this dichotomy between the two. While the former is representative of experimentation, yet, eventually concluding in concepts of a unified whole and hence, being representative of something; the latter tends towards a de-unification and disintegration. One of the most significant manifestations of this basic premise of Postmodernism is explicitly evident in the 'de-mystification' of the concept of truth. Erstwhile, truth was an absolute entity, albeit abstract and transcendental, as Saussure projects it, as meaning was synchronically fixed. Postmodernism, on the other hand, interrogated the very premise by re-nomenclaturing truth as itinerant. Men like Foucault and Derrida talked of "fictionalising of history" and "deferring of meaning", signaling a hiatus that was eventually developed by Baudrillard who conceived a post-modern world as one where the "simulacrum" is not bound to be an imitation of the real; rather, the real has to be a copy of the virtual.

However, just like the "global" and the "local", in spite of being apparently binary and contradictory, have a camaraderie, the "glocal", Postmodernism, too, bears an extension of the modern and also possesses a cultural context. As Lyotard opines, "What then is postmodern? What place, if any, does it occupy in that vertiginous work of questioning the rules that govern images and narratives? It is undoubtedly part of the modern" (378). As for the former, postmodernism is an extension of the modernist tendency of Formalism or New Criticism, in the form of "self-referentiality". Though this postmodern condition is a product of its distancing from any form of truth or fact, thereby leaving little scope for the postmodernist thought except delving into itself, this happens to be the first connecting link between the Modern and the Post-modern, given the Modernist affiliation and inclination towards "Closed Reading". The latter, offers the concrete link between the traditional lines of literary thought; *sans* Modernism, that vehemently counters the traditional; and postmodernism. Cultural context has been one of the affable and incipient factors that have contributed to the nailing down of meaning in a text and it is this "cultural context" which provides the required gravitas to the idea of a traditional continuity even in the Western Canon of Thought.

Andreas Huyssen indicates in the multifacetedness of the Postmodern Question when he asserts, "What needs further exploration is whether this transformation has generated genuinely new aesthetic forms in the various arts or whether it mainly recycles techniques and strategies of modernism itself, reinscribing them into an altered cultural context" (184). In the light of such contrasting points-of-view, juxtaposed against each other, in an attempt to delimit postmodernism, the entire construct seems to be falling asunder. However, if the entire postmodern period is studied chronologically, as a phase of development, bordering closely on metamorphosis, the juxtapositions seem merely superficial. The immediate decade, marking the very inception of the postmodern, i.e. the 1960s, emerges as a period of tumult in various streams of social life comprising arts, architecture, literature, etc. The new trend was esoteric, in that it rejected and criticised the tenets and facets of modernism. However, strangely, through the "cultural contexts", it was also establishing itself as a part of the tradition. An identical trait was found in the architecture of the 1960s, as Huyssen says, "...postmodern circles...favor a reintroduction of multivalent symbolic dimensions into architecture, a mixing of codes, an appropriation of local vernaculars and regional traditions" (189). The cultural codes and the native register that found a place in Postmodernism thus formed the foundational "cultural context" that prevented postmodernism from falling into the gyre of negation, chaos and absolute lack of firm ground, allegations that it bore in the wake of being anti-modern, thereby leaving scope for a possibility of completion.

However, the "*sans* modernism", as mentioned earlier, has its own debates and loopholes that centre around the 1970s, the phase when culture became an "amorphous and scattered" scene as compared to the 1960s. As a result of the decisive shift in the cultural context, the concept of the 1960s developed some ruptures, offering space to the pro-modern perspectives to creep into the postmodern. To quote Huyssen, "Modernist styles have actually not been abolished, but, as one art critic recently observed, continue, 'to enjoy a kind of half-life in mass culture,'..." (197).

In other words, the chronological Postmodern can be categorised into, as Huyssen opines, into the *avant garde* and the typical postmodern, with the latter being a composite of the Modern and the *avant garde*. The postmodern, then, beyond chronology, typically originates with the 1970s and carries the extensions of the Modern. Subsequent upon this, the traditional, Modern and the Post-modern, all seem to be inherently connected and twined in a continuous relationship, thereby interrogating successfully, the claim of the Western Canon of Thought working on the principle of Replacement.

Elaborating the argument, there are two ideas embedded in the framework that constructs the edifice of the previous paragraph: postmodern as an extension of the traditional and postmodern as an extension of the modern. The three stakeholders, the traditional, the modern and the postmodern, all work together, like clockwork, creating a chain of thought and interpretation. A sweeping, yet eidetic, look across the canon of Western Literary Thought shall ascertain the connect. The traditional concept of literary creations has been orchestrated by an assemblage of the particular and the universal in a search for meaning. The Modern, too, much like the traditional, vouched and strove for a decisive universal meaning, albeit through the specificities of Closed Reading. The Postmodern, the new development of the 1960s, seeks meaning, the universal, through the particular, which invariably is the cultural context.

The "cultural context" also draws validity and authenticity from the literary trends that have engulfed the Western Literary Canon since the Victorian Age. The trends find conception in realism, dealing with seeking meaning in social life; followed by Naturalism that seeks human anatomy and nature as the centre of meaning. Next came Stream of Consciousness that sought meaning in the workings of the conscious mind; and this led to Surrealism, focusing on the workings of the unconscious mind. Having exhausted the social and the individual, the general and the particular; literature, then, in the 1950s and 1960s, in sequence with postmodernism, re-ventured into the social, albeit in the new nomenclature of Cultural Studies, an insight into cultural contexts for deciphering meaning.

The entire construct of the traditional, modern and the postmodern is summarised in what Lyotard opines, "Thus understood, postmodernism is not modernism at its end, but in a nascent state, and this state is recurrent" (Lyotard, 378). Postmodernism, then, is not deconstruction all the way, but a revert to the traditional and cultural nuances that places the specificities of life at the fore, as against the universal, but leads to the universal through the particular.

However, much like T. S. Eliot avers in "Tradition and Individual Talent", every approach and critical methodology must have its uniqueness and salient features that define it, and postmodernism is not an exception to it. My personal forays, extremely limited, into the domain of the postmodern, have created a dimension, an outer frame, to borrow the vocabulary of painting, within which I perceive the entire construct of the postmodern. The one word that I use to define it is: Construction. The entire corpus and register of the postmodern is preoccupied with the idea of constructing, generating, rather than representing or re-presenting. A typical postmodern text establishes itself in the dominion of creating – a creation that does not, mandatorily, have to be a representation of the real, but a creation of the author's mind and perspective. However, having said that, postmodern criticism does not acknowledge the author, rather seeks references within the text to generate meaning. The avenues, superficially contradictory, do reconcile in the fact that the text is a construction, and hence its parameters are "within the text", rather than "without the text". This "self-referentiality" is at the core of the postmodern frame and fills most of the colours.

This self-referentiality and the absence of any external referent alters the relationship of the postmodern with "truth" as we know it and consequently, also interrogates the basic notion of literature being a "reflection" or imitation of the real. If a text ceases to have an external referent, it does not "belong" to any of the extra-textual truth or reality that, to us, exists as a matter of fact. The literary creation and the external world, then become two independent categories that have no apparent "connect" with each other. Moreover, this loss of belongingness leaves the text in an abyss that has no end, with the text a 'victim' to innumerable interpretations, even contradictory to one another.

However, the postmodern is not a negative spiral that it appears to be and this "relevance" is offered by Jean Baudrillard. In his article, "Simulacra and Simulations", he opines:

> …present-day simulators try to make the real, all the real, coincide with their simulation models. But…something has disappeared: the sovereign difference between them that was the abstraction's charm. For it is the difference which forms the poetry of the map and the charm of the territory, the magic of the concept and the charm of the real…With it goes all of metaphysics. No more mirror of being and appearances, of the real and its concept; no more imaginary coextensivity: rather, genetic miniaturisation is the dimension of simulation. The real is produced from miniaturised units, from matrices, memory banks and command models – and with these it can be reproduced an indefinite number of times. It no longer has to be rational, since it is no longer measured against some ideal or negative instance. It is nothing more than operational. In fact, since it is no longer enveloped by an imaginary, it is no longer real at all. It is a hyperreal: the product of an irradiating synthesis of combinatory models in a hyperspace without atmosphere (382).

The "territory" and the "map", used by Baudrillard, are analogous of the conventional real and the textual reference and the inverted relationship that the two share in the postmodern world. The term "hyperreal" summarises the entire construct of postmodernism. It forays into a world where the conventional relationship between the text and the real referent is compromised. This hypothesis, subsequently, interrogates all the principles of traditional rhetoric's because the text is not bound to fall-in-line with anything. In the absence of any "argument" to substantiate, the text becomes independent and this situation is summarised as "hyperreal" by Baudrillard. It is a world deracinated into an order wherein the text creates the referent or the real. In other words, literature and criticism, in postmodernism, enter into a disputatious space where the traditional notions of probability and rationality go a-begging. *Pro bono*, postmodernism offers an alternative word to accommodate its *amour fou*: "arational". The deliberate refraining from the notions of irrational is obviously understood, the term "arational" points towards an order of literature that, though different, is not altogether regressive or chaotic. As Baudrillard states, "Simulation is no longer that of a territory, a referential being or a substance. It is the generation by models of a real without origin or reality: a hyperreal" (382).

The modes of production also alter drastically in the wake of the "arational", holding tenuously and reticently to the orthodox. One of the several implications of the inculcation of this new order emerges in historical narratives as they become *sans* referent, thereby losing any historical or primitive representation that they averred. Fredric Jameson rightly says in "Foreword to Lyotard's *The Postmodern Condition*": "The Nietzschean 'strength to *forget* the past' – in preparation for the mutation of the superman to come – is here paradoxically redeployed as a property of storytelling itself, of precisely those narratives, heroic or other, in which we have been taught to see a form of primitive data storage or of social reproduction" (229-30).

An obvious question that raises its head, in the wake of deconstructing all the notions and concepts of "truth", "real" and even the historical, is: what impelled this paradigm shift leading to the inception of the Postmodern? The answer to it lies in the twentieth century itself, the first half, to be precise, and needs no deep reading as all the symptoms and malaises are visible at the very surface. The turmoil and chaos that culminated in the pandemonium of the Second World War and the twin bombings of Japan presents every germ sprouting into an evident disillusionment with the real and external world. While the Experimental Modernism was a product of the 'disillusionment' with realism, the Postmodern owes its genesis to disillusionment with "what was". The real and the concrete world outside, in the first three fortnights of the twentieth century, is a classical example of rapid social decadence. Three events of the twentieth century that stand at the zenith of "the times"' delinquencies were: First World War, The Great Economic Depression and the Second World War. While not delving into history and historiography, the events almost followed one after the other, engulfing the entire half-century into an eclipse that found no respite and reprieve in an already collapsing traditional order of things. American poet Randall Jarrell speaks of the loss and the ensuing bewilderment in *The Lost World* (1965):

> Whispering to myself the tale
> These shout – done with my schoolwork, I commence
> My real life: my arsenal, my workshop
> Opens, and in impotent omnipotence
> I put on the helmet and the breastplate Pop
> Cut out and soldered for me. Here is the shield
> I sawed from beaver board and painted; here on top
> The bow that only Odysseus can wield
> And eleven vermilion-ringed, goose-feathered arrows.
> (The twelfth was broken on the battlefield
> When, searching among snap beans and potatoes,
> I stepped on it.) Some dry weeds, a dead cane
> Are my spears. The knife on the bureau's
> My throwing-knife; the small unpainted biplane
> Without wheels – that so often, helped by human hands,
> Has taken off from, landed on, the counterpane –
> Is my Spad. (37)

The postmodern, then, is a resistance to the rampant 'lawlessness' that pervaded the "modern order"; an effort to seek an alternative "centre" to replace the "centre that could no longer hold". In the absence of a concrete framework to counter and negate the Modernist chaos, the postmodern was born and as a 'repulsion' from the prevailing "real", sought an alternative "real" and "true", one that could then be created in the physical world. In other words, the simulation became the creator of the actual: the parameters that the simulation determined were attempted to be realised in the actual world.

However, the chronological Modern Era also heralded the dawn of the post-colonial era in various nations and the tendency stretched well into the chronological postmodern. The independence of Ireland, the Russian war of Independence and the independence of India are examples in case. The post-colonial marked the zenith of the ideologies of the subaltern as they got the liberty of expressing themselves independently as the yoke of oppressive regimes ended. With the progression of time, this Post-colonial perspective and the intertwined ascent of the Subaltern Studies exemplified the "representation of culture" into postmodern literature. The very concept, by virtue of it being a "representation" of cultural contexts countered the predominant postmodern strains. The post-colonial and Subaltern Studies, then, do carry the common denominator of Postmodernism, albeit chronologically. In the ensuing order of assimilative postmodernism, the former becomes the "other" to the predominant tenets of the postmodern. Analysing the entire construct carefully, a search for a "new truth" is the common factor underlying the corpus of the "self" and the "other" of Postmodernism. However, what is critical is that the "new truth" that is sought by both differ singularly. While the "self" is obsessed with the notion of a philosophical truth, one that transcends the traditional order and encompasses the entire new construct; the "other" seeks for a culture specific truth, an order that is not only traditional, practiced by a community since ages, but equally novel. However, by virtue of the magnitude of the truth sought by the "self" in contrast to the 'puny' truth of the "other", the relationship between the two continues to be dyadic.

America and Postmodernism

The United States of America marked its first 'global' presence with the migration of the British to America, in the seventeenth century. Along with the British, the ones who 'displaced' the aboriginal tribes in the USA, were Europeans. These migrants, primarily constituted the 'castaways', evading penalisation and harrying, and formed the first 'civilised' inhabitants in an otherwise richly populated land: "North America was sporadically settled by Europeans in the sixteenth century, and by large numbers of English settlers, many of them fleeting from religious or political persecution, from the early seventeenth century onwards" (Sen 1).

The migration of the British, establishing the New England along the Eastern periphery of the USA, paved the way for an aggressive colonisation and domination of the land, a domination that ended with the Declaration of Independence in 1776. Ironical, as Krishna Sen says, "The English settlers wrested independence from England in 1776" (1), the USA was a child of Britishers who settled in the land that was eventually named as The United States of America. Owing to this history of origins, in migrations and the already residing aboriginals, heterogeneity, since the very inception of the USA, became one of its critical positions and reality. Subsequent upon this heterogeneity, multicultural and multi-ethnicity became the defining characteristics of the USA.

Literature, correspondingly, adopted the multi-dimensionality of the nation, but the journey was long and uphill for till the latter half of the nineteenth century, American Literature was the "other" in the huge web of World Literatures. It had, to its credit, only one 'virtue': being an extension of English Literature. There were two major arguments for this debacle: First, that it was composed in a language of the British; and secondly, that it lacked its own aesthetic artifice. It took a long time for American Literature to wrest its due from these allegations and there were several watershed moments in this long crusade: In 1783, Noah Webster published *American Spelling Book* attempting an American English to 'supersede' British English. English being the language common to both the nations, Webster modified spellings to distinguish American English from British English. He followed it with his more radical book *American Dictionary of the English Language*, published in 1828, that carried abundant words from outside English of England. Samuel Knapp, in 1829, published *Lectures on American Literature, with Remarks on Some Passages of American History*, a compendium of American literature, oratory, painting and scientific treatises.

The three texts, re-visited in contemporaneity, are classical representations of nation building discourses, giving a decisive direction to the construct of The United States of America as a nation. D. H. Lawrence, in *Studies in Classical American Literature*, in 1923, moved beyond into the construct of American Literature, detonating the entire esoteric dialectic of European literature. Not only did Lawrence absolve the hitherto American Literature, he also furrowed into the edifice of European literary knowledge system that had "...conceived [America] in the European imagination before it was recorded as a written fact in its literature" (Sengupta 29), thereby exposing their inability to comprehend American Literature:

> We like to think of the old-fashioned American classics as children's books. Just childishness, on our part. The old American art-speech contains an alien quality, which belongs to the American continent and to nowhere else. But, of course, so long as we insist on reading the books as children's tales, we miss all that. One wonders what the proper high-brow Romans of the third and fourth or later centuries read into the strange utterances of Lucretius or Apuleius or Tertullian, Augustine or Athanasius. The uncanny voice of Iberian Spain, the weirdness of old Carthage, the passion of Libya and North Africa; you may bet the proper old Romans never heard these at all. They read old Latin inference over the top of it, as we read old European inference over the top of Poe or Hawthorne. It is hard to hear a new voice, as hard as it is to listen to an unknown language. We just don't listen. There is a new voice in the old American classics. The world has declined to hear it, and has blabbed about children's stories. Why? – Out of fear. The world fears a new experience more than it fears anything. Because a new experience displaces so many old experiences. And it is like trying to use muscles that have perhaps

> never been used, or that have been going stiff for ages. It hurts horribly. The world doesn't fear a new idea. It can pigeon-hole any idea. But it can't pigeon-hole a real new experience. It can only dodge. The world is a great dodger, and the Americans the greatest. Because they dodge their own very selves. (7)

The entire socio-literary discourse was eventually capped by James Truslow Adams in *The Epic of America* (1931), when he coined the term "American Dream". It was the epitome of the erstwhile American nationalist and literary discourses. The term, though, has been subject to multiple interpretations, varying from jingoism to materialistic pursuit; it originally was coined by Adams to demarcate a "global" American glory:

> ...American dream of a better, richer, and happier life for all our citisens of every rank which is the greatest contribution we have as yet made to the thought and welfare of the world. That dream or hope has been present from the start. Ever since we became an independent nation, each generation has seen an uprising of the ordinary Americans to save that dream from the forces which appeared to be overwhelming and dispelling it. Possibly the greatest of these struggles lies just ahead of us at this present time – not a struggle of revolutionists against established order, but of the ordinary man to hold fast to those rights to "life, liberty, and the pursuit of happiness" which were vouchsafed to us in the past in vision and on parchment. (viii)

It was the time when industrialisation and urbanisation had already made decisive inroads into the fabric of traditional America and, as a direct outcome, also affected the literary modes of representation producing poets like Frost, seeking nature, and dramatists like Tennessee Williams, concentrating on the repercussions of a rampant Industrial Revolution and modernisation, in texts like *A Streetcar Named Desire* (1947). The concept of the "American Dream", however, in its aftermath, suffered a blow, further intensified by the "others" in American life and literature, who leaned, often audaciously, in favour of its criticism: Arthur Miller being one example of the former, while Toni Morrison of the latter.

The advent of Industrialisation, however, catalysed the transition, of American Literature, from Naturalism towards Modernism. While Realism and Naturalism were phenomena hovering around the centrality of a national discourse, Modernism, in its experimental pursuit of universality, swiftly, chartered a distinct discourse that negates the constructs of a national discourse. The penchant for "global aspirations" (130), as Ashok Sengupta calls it, overtakes the nationalistic discourse that underlined the realistic and naturalistic registers of American Literature. One of the greatest proponents of American Modernism, Henry James, once opined:

> I aspire to write in such a way that it would be impossible to the outsider to say whether I am at a given moment an American writing about England or an Englishman writing about America (dealing as I do with both countries), and so far from being ashamed of such ambiguity I should be exceedingly proud of it, for it would be highly civilised" (Qtd. in Sengupta, "From Howell" 132)

The quote points, abundantly, at the increasing inclination towards the universal. However, Henry James himself, also inclines towards the American discourse in Modern Literature. A character says in *A Portrait of a Lady*: "Ah, one doesn't give up one's country any more than one gives *up* one's grandmother. They're both antecedent to choice – elements of one's composition are not to be eliminated" (64). The Modern impulse, then, in American Literature, is a combination of the universal and the national.

In spite of the criticism that the American Value System and the Great American Dream was exposed to, till the 1950s, the social order, tenaciously stuck to the principle of conformity with social disagreements commencing, significantly, with Rosa Parks' vehement refusal to vacate her seat in favour of reserved seats for Black people, in 1955. The entire corpus of American life, principally beyond the 1950s, when the immediate impact of World War II was over, underwent a paradigmatic change, becoming explicit with consumerism and its sensibilities. The Mass society that emerged beyond the 1950s, was merely a pastiche of media culture and products available in the consumerist market: America had entered the Post-Industrial domain.

The Literary Postmodern in American Literature, in tandem, emerged, deriding what was 'obvious' in Modernism. One of the foremost consequences was the eradication of the principle of High and Low Literature in favour of, to use a term from culture, "popular" literature. Literature became a representative of a constructed world, in contrast to the "perspectivised" world of Modernism. This constructed world, in literature, offered the 'ideal' to be simulated in the actual physical world. The pastiche, grew in literary representations, and, intermittently stretched into parody, albeit not in the derogatory sense inherently, but as a mode of representing nonconforming themes, such as uncharacteristic sexuality. Henry Miller stands a classic example of such topics smacking of 'apocryphal' quality on Modernist terminology, whose book *Tropic of Cancer* underwent severe scrutiny in the U.S. for its sexual content.

America, having overcome the setbacks that it received in the first half of the 20th century, reflected the same in its literature. Aided by 'its own' English, and the concurrent technological communicative devices and language, American Literature, with its post-modernity, stamped its authority on the schema of world literature:

> American culture, aided by possession both of the English language, the main world language, and the newer languages of communications technology, reaches everywhere, whether it is popular, serious, seriopopular or any mixture of both. American writing has reflected this position of power, growing more open to history, to the global proliferation of styles and forms, to the sometimes exhilarating and sometimes depressing new span of human curiosity. (Bradbury 370)

It is pertinent to mention, briefly, the social scenarios in America between the two time frames elaborated earlier: the immediacy of the Second World War and the time when the immediate impact of the War was over. America's bombing of Hiroshima and Nagasaki, effectively ending the World War, not only caused ripples in world politics, but also carved on stone, the ambition of America as a nation. The message of superiority, however, was modified to "friendly superiority", as America went on to assist its erstwhile enemies in their nation re-building. In addition, the 'unattacked' industrial order of America, in the war, was fed with educated American youth, leading to a blossoming post-Industrial America.

However, the picture was not as bright as it showed and this, 'digression' is explicitly referred to by Allen Ginsberg in his seminal poem "Howl":

> What sphinx of cement and aluminum bashed open their skulls and ate up their brains and imagination?
> Moloch! Solitude! Filth! Ugliness! Ashcans and unobtainable dollars! Children screaming under the stairways! Boys sobbing in armies! Old men weeping in the parks!
> Moloch! Moloch! Nightmare of Moloch! Moloch the loveless! Mental Moloch! Moloch the heavy judger of men!
> Moloch the incomprehensible prison! Moloch the crossbone soulless jailhouse and Congress of sorrows! Moloch whose buildings are judgment! Moloch the vast stone of war! Moloch the stunned governments!
> Moloch whose mind is pure machinery! Moloch whose blood is running money! Moloch whose fingers are ten armies! Moloch whose breast is a cannibal dynamo! Moloch whose ear is a smoking tomb!
> Moloch whose eyes are a thousand blind windows! Moloch whose skyscrapers stand in the long streets like endless Jehovahs! Moloch whose factories

> dream and croak in the fog! Moloch whose smoke-stacks and antennae crown the cities!
> Moloch whose love is endless oil and stone! Moloch whose soul is electricity and banks! Moloch whose poverty is the specter of genius! Moloch whose fate is a cloud of sexless hydrogen! Moloch whose name is the Mind! (182)

Published in the year 1956, in his collection of poems *Howl and Other Poems*, his was a scathing attack at the apparent affluency of America. Ginsberg himself stands as the representative of the Beat Generation, one of the foremost literary movements that mark the advent of Post-modernism in American literature. The poem proved to be a precursor to the political and social turmoils and the resistance to it that defined the subsequent literatures of America.

One significant aspect of American Post-modernism is the new kind of nation building discourse that glorifies the multicultural and multiethnic nature of America. Leslie Marmon Silko and Robert Haydon are sparkling examples of literature's acknowledgement of America's newfound multifarious nature. While Silko, an aboriginal, insists on the significance of American cultural values and nuances; Haydon, the first African American poet Laureate of the U.S., speaks vociferously of the global human and humaneness. Silko, in her celebrated novel *Ceremony* says, approaching indigenous cultures: "As long as the hummingbird had not abandoned the land, somewhere there were still flowers, and they could all go on"; while Haydon's title poem in *Words in the Mourning Time*, says:

> Reclaim now, now renew the vision of
> a human world where godliness
> is possible and man
> is neither gook nigger honkey wop or kike
> but man
> permitted to be man. (www.goodreads.com)

While the papers that have been contributed for the anthology cover the disparate thematic, formal and theoretical paraphernalia that comprises the American Post-modern, I have tried to delve, briefly, into the salient attributes of Post-modernism and its position in America. It can be safely left to the papers to address the multi-dimensionality of the post-modern in American literature. To conclude my naïve remarks on post-modernism and post-modernism in American Literature, it is pertinent to foreground and acknowledge that the celebrated principles of post-modernism and its application to American Literature wrest on the social paradigm that it 'apparently' decries and demolishes. In other words, the very idea of society influencing literature and vice-versa is at full display in the literary manifestation of post-modern literary principles. It is also important to understand this perspective because in contemporaneity, the scene in American Literature is, controversially, hanging between the Post-modern and the Post Post-modern. While the wave of virtual reality and post-truth has overtaken self-reflexivity and principle of the simulacra of the Post-modern, it is equally valid that the post post-modern is still in its nascent stage. Consequently, clarity of the post-modern principles shall go a long way in understanding the domain of the post post-modern:

> But in privileging disorder, theorists cannot extract themselves from the weight of their disciplinary traditions, even if they want to...Thus there arise complex layerings in which traces of old paradigms are embedded within new, resistances to mastery are enfolded with impulses toward mastery, totalising moves are made in the service of local knowledge… (Hayles 265)

Works Cited

Adams, James Truslow. *The Epic of America*. Little, Brown, and Company, 1931. ia601607.us.archive.org/1/items/in.ernet.dli.2015.262385/2015.262385.The-Epic. pdf. Accessed 3 April 2021.

Baudrillard, Jean. "Simulacra and Simulations." *Literary Theories: A Reader and Guide*, edited by Julian Wolfreys, Edinburgh UP, 1999, pp. 381-94.

Berke, Amy, Robert R. Bleil, Jordan Cofer and Doug Davis. *Writing the Nation: A Concise Introduction to American Literature, 1865 to Present*. U of North Georgia P, 2015.

Bradbury, Malcolm and Richard Ruland. *From Puritanism to Post-modernism: A History of American Literature*. Penguin Books, 1992.

Ginsberg, Allen. "Howl". *The New Anthology of American Poetry: Postmodernisms, 1950-Present,* edited by Steven Gould Axelord, et al. Rutgers UP, 2012.

Haydon, Robert. "Words in the Mourning Time". www.goodreads.com. Accessed 23 May 2021.

Hayles, N. Katherine. "Conclusion: Chaos and Culture: Postmodernism(s) and the Denaturing of Experience Book." *Chaos Bound: Orderly Disorder in Contemporary Literature and Science Book*. Cornell UP, pp. 265-95.

Horace. *The Satires, Epistles and Ars Poetica*. Translated by A. S. Kline, 2005.

Huyssen, Andreas. "Mapping the Postmodern." *Postmodernism: Critical Concepts*. Vol II, *Critical Texts*, edited by Victor E. Taylor and Charles E. Winquist. Routledge, 1998.

James, Henry. *A Protrait of a Lady. Bartleby,* www.bartleby.com/ebook/adobe/311.pdf. Accessed 3 April 2021.

Jameson, Fredric. "Foreword to Lyotard's *The Postmodern Condition*." *Postmodernism: Critical Concepts*. Vol II *Critical Concepts,* edited by Victor E. Taylor and Charles E. Winquist, Routledge, 1998.

Jarrel, Randall. *The Lost World*. www.poemhumter.com. Accessed 20 July 2021.

Lawrence, D. H. *Studies in Classical American Literature*. Martin Secker, 1920. ia801901.us.archive.org/2/items/in.ernet.dli.2015.96447/2015.96447.Studies-In-Classic-American-Literature_text.pdf. Accessed 3 April 2021.

Lyotard, Jean-Francois. "Answer to the Question, What is Postmodern." *Literary Theories: A Reader and Guide*, edited by Julian Wolfreys, Edinburgh UP, 1999, pp 371-80.

Sen, Krishna & Ashok Sengupta, editors. *A Short History of American Literature*. Orient Blackswan, 2017.

Sen, Krishna. "The History and Culture of the United States of America." Sen & Sengupta, pp. 1-28.

Sengupta, Ashok. "From Howells to Miller: Realism, Naturalism, Regionalism and Modernism." Sen & Sengupta, pp. 106-74.

---. "From the Early Narratives to the Colonial Era". Sen & Sengupta, pp. 29-58.

Wain, Leah. "Introduction: Postmodernism? Not Representing Postmodernism." *Literary Theories: A Reader and Guide*, edited by Julian Wolfreys, Edinburgh UP, 1999, pp. 359-70.

CHAPTER 1

Sexual Innuendo in John Barth's *Lost in the Funhouse*: Metafictional Interpolations

Harpreet Kaur Vohra

Patricia Waugh in her book *Metafiction: The Theory and Practice of Self-Conscious Fiction* (1984), defines metafiction as "a term given to fictional writing which self-consciously and systematically draws attention to its status as an artifact in order to pose questions about the relationship between fiction and reality. In providing a critique of their own methods of construction, such writings not only examine fundamental structures of narrative fiction, they also explore the possible fictionality of the world outside the literary fictional text" (2). This postmodern technique has both the playfulness and dimension to elaborate upon an experience beyond the conventional paradigms of familiarity. The self-referential dimension of literary modernism consisted partly in rejecting all forms of traditional narrative like unity, transparency, linearity and realism and replaced it with diffusion, opaque language and alienation (Currie Intro vi). Metafictional interpolations in fiction brought about not only self-reflexivity towards the creation of the text; it also gave much freedom to the artist/writer to go beyond the conventionalities of accepted forms of expression. Metafictional elements have been used in literature for a very long time: Cervantes' novel *Don Quixote* is metafictional as it raises questions about the nature of fiction itself; *The Divine Comedy* can easily pass off as surfiction as the narrator enters the text, while *The Canterbury Tales* consists of a group of pilgrims telling their own stories as part of a contest to win a free meal. The self-reflexivity in the novels and the close examination of the art of fiction makes metafiction a sounding board, where both the craft and the negotiations by the craftsman come to focus, thereby laying bare several preconceived notions about "how" a novel is to be written. Like Waugh says in her book, *The Theory and Practice of Self-Conscious Fiction,* "Metafictional novels tend to be constructed on the principle of a fundamental and sustained opposition: the construction of a fictional illusion…and the laying bare of that illusion" (6). So how is sex treated in a postmodern text? And how is teenage sexuality and its attendant complexities dealt with? Does sex and its innuendoes in postmodern texts lay bare the illusions related to them? Or does it merely rework ideas related to sex into fancy undecipherable images?

Barth described the self-reflexive novel as, "self-conscious, vertiginously arch, fashionably solipsistic, unoriginal – in fact a convention of twentieth-century literature. Another story about a writer writing a story!" (Bell 88). When John Barth wrote *Lost in the Funhouse* in 1968 much was made out about the metafictional elements of the work. The highly plastic style, the sexual images and the discovery of the self in an otherwise highly diffused medium made the work interesting to critics who made both glowing and wild interpretations about the coming-of-age tale. The journey of Ambrose to the funhouse and the concomitant details of both sexual encounter and family outing, bring together varied planes of experience with naïve hero and femme fatale encounters. What strikes most readers are echoed in a review of the book in *The New York Times*, when the reviewer introduces the work as, "[T]his new and thoroughly confusing book…" (Davenport 1968). The manner in which Barth tells the story lucidly blurs lines between the real and imaginary while at the same time firmly establishing a style which was to become his own. *Lost in the Funhouse* teases the reader and makes her re-imagine what a story can be and how it could be told. The funhouse which is an American conceptualisation of an amusement park consists of trick mirrors, shifting floors and other devices to scare or amuse people as they walked through. So, when Barth chooses the funhouse as the site of his metafictional work, the very premise of the amusement park, even in terms of physicality is apparently an ideal location to parallel the many disjunctions, detours, false appearances and interpolations that mark a postmodern work. The metafictional elements in the work also amplify the effect of the trick mirrors and shifting floors which act as fertile ground to negotiate what reality is and how is it interred in metaphor and idiom of the story. Barths's metafictional work primarily falls under the category of surfiction (even though a couple of other categories can be attributed to it) wherein the narrator enters the text. Raymond Federman's book *Surfiction* discusses "the mode in terms of overt narratorial intrusion so that, as in the 'self-begetting novel', the focus appears to be on the ironist him/herself rather than the overt and covert levels of ironic text" (Waugh 14).

Metafiction as a postmodern device has often punctured narrative; sometimes confusing readers as they have to negotiate between the real and the apparent while challenging their sensibilities at most other times. It sometimes becomes a tantalising device which can even take away from the seriousness of the plot and Barth has often been accused as being too self-referential and self-reflexive, thus making his works sometimes difficult to understand. Barth had perhaps never imagined that his works would initiate vociferous discussions about both the craft of writing and the onus that the creator takes towards her work. But the strength of randomness of metafiction is what gives Barth the ability to play with language and disrupt it so easily at the same time. Peter Stoicheff, in this regard says, that the system of metafictional text is creative as well as unstable, producing what Barthes(sic) terms the "jouissance" of an inexhaustible possibility of interpretations (Hayles 87). Metafiction, hence has within it, the possibility of umpteen and highly complex interpretations. Metafiction is ubiquitous in mid-twentieth century American fiction. John Barth in his preface to the 1987 Anchor reprint of *Lost in the Funhouse* made it clear that a barrage of factors like "post-1945 cultural and epistemological issues in the United States, poststructuralism in high theory and postcolonial and race politics outside the academy together with the success of the US culture industry…unhinged American authors faith in mimesis and what a reality unmediated by images, language and ideology could be" (Duvall 17). So, for Barth to employ an apparently playful and yet highly complex narrative was the result of the churnings in American society post-World War II and its concomitant effects on expression in literature. Waugh quotes Philip Roth as he describes the American novelists of the twentieth century who were completely immersed in "trying to understand, describe, and then make credible much of American reality" (9). He then makes a hard-hitting comment when he says that the American reality was so complex that it "stupefies, it sickens, it infuriates, and finally it is a kind of embarrassment to one's own meager imagination. The actuality is continually outdoing our talents" (9). Waugh says that Barth's *Lost in the Funhouse* is clearly self-begetting, surfictional and metafictional (14) as it is an account of the development of a character to the point where he is able to compose the novel we have just finished reading (self-begetting); the entry of the narrator into the text (surfiction); and employment of fictional writing which self-consciously and systematically draws attention to its status as an artifact to pose questions about the relationship between fiction and reality (metafiction).

Barth constantly talks about the craft of creating a story in the tale: from the reference to the use of italics for "oral emphasis" to the nineteenth-century fictional convention of initials and blanks substituted for proper names to the description of physical appearance and mannerisms as a method of characterisation and the use of the first-person narrative to diving as a literary symbol. All these metafictional interpolations make their way into the story – sometimes staccato and other times mellifluous, almost blending into the story.

The opening lines of the story point to what the funhouse isn't a place for naïve fun: a children's amusement park. Ambrose understands very early in the story that the funhouse is not meant for him but for lovers, "For whom is the funhouse fun? For Ambrose it is *a place of fear and confusion*" (*Lost in the Funhouse* 59). Ambrose is at an age when he is beset by all kinds of insecurities about his body, his sexual abilities, his voice and his appeal to the opposite sex. On the other hand, his brother Peter who is fifteen and their friend Magda who is fourteen are not apparently affected by any of this identity/self/sexual/vocal/bodily questions at all. In fact their friend is repeatedly described thus: "Magda's figure was exceedingly well developed for her age" (*Lost in the Funhouse* 65). Her well-developed figure, her brassiere-strap, her billowing skirt and her playing Nigger and Master only prepare the reader to read what goes on in the funhouse as sexual adventure. "In the tumbling – barrel, too, just inside the Devil's mouth entrance to the funhouse, the girls were upended and their boyfriends and others could see up their dresses if they cared to. Which was the whole point, Ambrose realised. Of the entire funhouse" (*Lost in the Funhouse* 71). The story is replete with sexual references and sex becomes a metaphor for language. "Ambrose gets hard when Ambrose doesn't want to, and obversely" (*Lost in the Funhouse* 68). Bauman Sygmunt opines that the triad of sex, eroticism and love has varied contexts as sex is natural and limited in forms while love and eroticism are "cultural products infinite in their expressions and applications." He says that "the postmodern novelty is emancipation of eroticism from both sexual reproduction and love" and hence allowing it the freedom to perform many new tasks including "the renegotiation of social relations inside the family and in public space, as well as new forms of identity" (Zygmunt Abstract).

Barth uses sexual metaphor to do all of these and more, by foregrounding the experience of Ambrose to run parallel with both the angst and the satisfaction of a writer crafting his fiction. Galloway says that Barth "applies a sexual analogy to the process of literary creation: male hegemony leads to artistic control and fruition" (Galloway 43). The preponderance of the image of sex as a metaphor of creation fills the pages of the story, often taking it to ludicrous heights: "The word *fuck* suggests suction and/or and/or flatulence" (*Lost in the Funhouse* 64) and the story of origin of lineage is full of incredible descriptions which make it ludicrous and highly imaginative at the same time. "...five hundred twelve women – English, Welsh, Bavarian, Swiss-of every class and every character, received unto themselves the penises the intromittent organs of five hundred twelve ancestors of the two hundred fifty-six ancestors of the etcetera..." (*Lost in the Funhouse* 64). Some lines later, in the same vein, the description of coitus, "The sluppish whisper, continuous as sea-wash round the globe, tide like falls and rises with the circuit of dawn and dusk" (*Lost in the Funhouse* 64). The descriptions of sexual acts, erotic feelings and sexual abandon make the work seep with a certain sexual idiom in which language and sex become each other's mirror. What does Barth want to tell the readers about narrative and how do the sexual idioms inform us about the trajectories in the story?

For the paper, three aspects related to sexual encounter and sexual metaphor are examined in order to decipher how metafictional interpolations prove to be larger commentaries on the craft of writing. The first is the examination of adolescent sexuality in terms of Ambrose, Magda and Peter; the second is the seemingly innocent game of Niggers and Masters and the third is the structure and games of the funhouse which point to a complete sexual construction, according to Barth. Adolescent sexuality is an important part of the story and the outing of three teenagers to the funhouse only acts as a framework upon which the triumvirate of identity, sexuality and experience gets propped up through the triangulation of narrator, author and protagonist. Barth teasingly tells the reader that everyone is bored of such teenage stories and yet he narrates it throughout the length of the story! The discovery of the marvels and the darkness of the body along with the attendant mixed feelings bring Ambrose to a point where he realises his inferiority in comparison to his brother Peter. The constant reference to Magda as a well built girl and the subsequent fear that she would be sexually attractive to Peter who was physically more macho than him makes the visit to the funhouse a complete fright.

The question of adolescent sexuality is a central concern of the story as three teenagers are discovering sexuality even as they sit in the car on way to the funhouse. Most descriptions have sexual overtones. Magda sits between the two boys, sweat patches can be seen on her armpits, she holds a banana as a prize which was "something hard to get nowadays" and how she "demonstrated her ability to hold a banana in one hand and peel it with her teeth" (*Lost in the Funhouse* 62) and the constant fear that Ambrose has of Magda who could accidentally sit on his hand. The metafictional interpolations in the sexual innuendoes amplify both the preoccupation with sex and the angst that it represented at the time in America. The flux in gender relations was accelerated during the World War II. Women were dramatically moving out of traditional roles due to war mobilisation and yet one could "discern signs of intense cultural anxiety about sex, gender and marriage" (Irvine 16) during this period. Magda, with her physical development and knowledge of the sway that she has over the boys is clearly assuming a role different from that of a diffident recipient who has to accept missionary positions and traditional ideas about sex. Even through all the infantilisation that the boys' mother does in conversation and games, all the metaphors are highly sexual in nature.

The metafictional reference in terms of the voice in the story, for example, also leads to one of the flashpoints of the narrative: the game of Niggers and Masters. Note how Barth uses metafiction when he talks about how a story should be presented: "The more closely an author identifies with the narrator, literally or metaphorically, the less advisable it is, as a rule, to use the first person narrative viewpoint" (*Lost in the Funhouse* 63). As John Barth made clear in his preface to the 1987 Anchor reprint of *Lost in the Funhouse*, the combined force of post-1945 cultural and epistemological crisis in the US, structuralism in high theory and postcolonialism and race politics outside the academy along with the success of the US culture industry, was enough to "fundamentally unhinge American authors faith in mimesis and what a reality unmediated by images, language and ideology could be" (Duvall 16). As a result, this sensibility turned the "critique of language representation inward towards America's cultural revolution and culture industry" (Duvall 17). The employment of the uncommon and sometimes even bizarre style of narrating the story perhaps was born of this flux in American life and culture: the metafictonal interpolations are perhaps only one of these many manifestations of the angst. Barth discusses the oral sexual encounter experienced by Ambrose where Magda assumed the role of the slave in the torture chamber. Even though Magda plays the role of the slave, she gets the better of her master by giving him an oral sexual experience as penance. Even though Ambrose was afraid to 'punish Magda alone "she led him to the whitewashed Torture Chambers...in the Slaves Quarters; there she knelt sweating among the bamboo rakes...pleadingly embraced his knees and...purchased clemency at a surprising price set by herself" (*Lost in the Funhouse* 63). Ambrose is unable to forget the "least detail of his life." Magda knows the power games and uses sex as a tool to balance the unequal power structures in the Master/Slave narrative. Magda, even though she's just fifteen knows how to evade the punishment even while she role-plays the slave because she discovers the power of sex and the apparent impuissance of Ambrose in the face of his first oral sexual encounter.

Barth uses metafictional interpolations when he discusses the structure of a story on the lines of Gustav Freytag's pyramid. He develops a scholarly theory on what should be expected in a story when he says, "The function of the beginning of the story is to introduce the principal characters, establish their initial relationships....The middle would narrate all relevant events from the time he loses his way" (*Lost in the Funhouse* 62). Barth then lends this pragmatic, matter-of-fact discussion a sexual colour when he says, "middles have the double and contradictory function of delaying the climax while at the same time preparing the reader for it and fetching him to it" (*Lost in the Funhouse* 62). The structure of the story itself is likened to the sexual act with its beginning and climax which is deliberately delayed. The reference to rising action is presented within quotations as "rising action", not to mean so much one of the tenets of Freytag but rather sexual action. Barth cleverly uses Freytag's terms to mimic the sexual act itself.

The reference to Fat May, the Laughing Lady in the funhouse, the image of the loose-toga'd lady on the empty cigar box and the many references to spermatozoa bring the sexual innuendoes to centre stage. The manner in which Fat May invites visitors to the funhouse is full of bawdy syntax, "Fat May mechanically shook, rocked on her heels, slapped her thighs while recorded laughter-uproarious, female...chuckled, wheezed, wept; tittered, groaned, exploded raucous and anew" (*Lost in the Funhouse* 64). The sensual toga along with a sea side view and the image of a lyre all act as a prelude to sex while the funny references to sperm heighten the complexion of the sexual narrative, "Can spermatozoa properly be thought of as male animalcules when they are no female spermatozoa? They grope through hot, dark windings, past Love's Tunnel's fearsome obstacles. Some perhaps lose their way" (*Lost in the Funhouse* 64). Even the reference to Magda's figure has a sexual reference in terms of increasing breast size, "she was remarkably well developed for her age; it was said that that came from rubbing with a Turkish towel, and there were other theories" (*Lost in the Funhouse* 65). Then the reference to Ambrose being glad that he hadn't gone swimming because "the cold water shrank you up so" (*Lost in the Funhouse* 66), (what is really shrinking here?). The consistent sexual overtones of the story through surfictional devices and the frequent references to the craft of creation of the story put the sexual metaphors at pivotal positions in the story.

There are two references to sexual innuendo in the story which have in themselves the echoes of both metaphorical sexual mischief of the funhouse as well as teenage sexuality becoming fertile ground to perceive the erotic in everything even as naïve as a fortune-telling machine or a mannequin. "If you knew your way in the funhouse like your own bedroom, you could wait until a girl came along and then slip away without ever getting caught, even if her boyfriend was right with her" (*Lost in the Funhouse* 66). The reference to clandestine sex in the alleys of the funhouse and not getting caught even though the act appears pretty blatant showcases the funhouse as a place of innumerable possibilities. Similarly, the reference to the mannequin and loneliness, "If a man lived by himself, he could take a department-store mannequin with flexible joints and modify her in certain ways. *However*, by the time he was that old he'd have a real woman" (*Lost in the Funhouse* 68). Also when Ambrose thinks of Magda, he imagines that her well-developed breasts were an indication that she would produce large amounts of milk. Similarly, Ambrose realises that the girls' upended skirts was the whole point of the funhouse and sex was the primary concern of the amusement park, "If you had X-ray eyes and could see everything going on at that instant under the boardwalk and in all the hotel rooms and cars and alleyways, you'd realise that all that normally *showed*, like restaurants and dance halls and clothing and test-your-strength machines, was merely preparation for intermission" (*Lost in the Funhouse* 71). All the references are to the sexual act which becomes the metaphor for language and action and personality all rolled into one. The tale is undoubtedly the story of Ambrose as an artist, a creator whose sensibilities do go beyond the mundane even as we watch him negotiate everyday conundrums. Jan Marta says that Ambrose "does not hate love but leaves it aside in his decision to be an artist." He will be a creator of funhouses "in their literary context, rather than a lover-appreciator of them in their sexual aspect."(Marta 212).

Lost in the Funhouse, with all its twists and turns, proves through its metafictional elements and sexual metaphor that the ways in which a story can be told has no boundaries. The constant references to sexual innuendo permeate the narrative to not just make it a tale about teenage identity and sexuality but also to comment on how sex just becomes a metaphor for language. The metafictional elements in the story form the framework through which all wordplay and sexual references organically make their way into the narrative. The setting of the funhouse proves to be an ideal site for this postmodern tale where the sexual implications and the linguistic representations form a rubric that becomes the framework of the story. To end with Patricia Waugh's explanation of 'meta', she says that it is required in order to explore the relationship between the arbitrary linguistic system and the world to which it apparently refers. "In fiction they are required in order to explore the relationship between the world of the fiction and the world outside fiction" (Waugh 3). This is what *Lost in the Funhouse* does with all its self-reflexivity and self-consciousness. And perhaps this line of the story sums up the whole exercise, "You think you're yourself, but there are other persons in you" (*Lost in the Funhouse* 68).

Works Cited

Barth, John. *Lost in the Funhouse.* Bantam, 1968.

Bell, M. Steven. "Literature, Self-Consciousness and Writing: The Example of Barth's *Lost in the Funhouse.*" *The International Fiction Review*, vol. 11, no. 9, 1984. pp. 84-89.

Currie, Mark, editor. *Metafiction.* Routledge, 1995.

Davenport, Guy. "Like Nothing Nameable." Review of *Lost in the Funhouse,* by John Barth. *The New York Times: on the Web.* 20 Oct, 1968, archive.nytimes.com/www.nytimes.com/books/98/06/21/specials/barth-funhouse.html

Duvall, John N, editor. "Postmodern Metafiction" by Amy J. Elias. *The Cambridge Companion to American Fiction after 1945.* Cambridge UP, 2012.

Galloway, Honora M.F. Rankina. "John Barth's Short Fiction: The Key to the Treasure is the Treasure." *Hungarian Studies in English*, vol. 16, 1983, pp. 43-49. *JSTOR*, www.jstor.org/stable/41273797.

Harris, Charles B. *Passionate Virtuosity: The Fiction of John Barth.* U of Illinois P, 1983.

Hayles, Katherine N, editor. *Chaos and Order: Complex Dynamics in Literature and Science.* U of Chicago P, 1991.

Irvine, Janice. M. *Disorders of Desire: Sexuality and Gender in Modern American Sexology.* Temple UP, 2005.

Marta, Jan. "John Barth's Portrait of the Artist as a Fiction: Modernism through the Looking Glass." *Canadian Review of Comparative Literature*, vol. 9, no. 2, 1982, pp. 208-22.

Waugh, Patricia. *The Theory and Practice of Self-Conscious Fiction.* Routledge, 1984.

Zygmunt, Bauman. "On Postmodern Uses of Sex." *Theory, Culture and Society*, vol. 15, no. 3-4, 1998, pp. 19-33, doi.org/10.1177/0263276498015003002.

CHAPTER 2

'Poo-tee-Weet': A Postmodern Reading of *Slaughterhouse Five*

Harsimran Kaur and *Shubham*

Kurt Vonnegut's *Slaughterhouse Five* is a blend of metafiction and historical fiction which allows frequent and deliberate use of allusions, historical documents, newspaper statements, and other literary text addressing the same issue. Literature always emerges as a by-product of the political, social, and religious upheavals that the period goes through. Patricia Waugh, in her work, *Metafiction: The Theory and Practice of Self-Conscious Fiction*, defines metafiction as, "fictional writing which self-consciously and systematically draws attention to its status as an artifact in order to pose questions about the relationship between fiction and reality" (2). Metafiction clearly puts the dichotomy of fantasy and real world in front of the readers and the narrative it builds alter and filter the reality which dilutes the ultimate authority of truth. The rejection of conventional plot and structured narrative style makes it digestible to the very end. Vonnegut juxtaposes the grand narrative of war and the horrors of bomb attack on Dresden by parallelly narrating about the 'other' world where Billy Pilgrim constantly visits and Tralfmadore, the life on which makes Billy ask, "How the inhabitants of a whole planet can live in peace!" (Vonnegut 95). The two contrasting worlds put up together by Vonnegut and beaded together by Billy Pilgrim provide satirical and ironical play to the plot. Being a time traveller, he keeps on visiting the Tralfmadorian land, which he says really exists and where he meets creatures that were, "two feet high, green, and shaped like plumber's friends. The creatures were friendly and they could see in four dimensions. They pitied Earthlings for being able to see only three" (Vonnegut 21).Vonnegut subsumes black humor through continuous use of irony throughout the narration. The fact that Billy being an Earthling can see through all directions and can travel back and forth, for, he has seen his marriage as well as the way his death will encounter him. The author ironically comments at the identity crisis of Billy, because he associates himself as much as with Tralfmadorian land as with planet Earth, hints at the psychological trauma of being a prisoner of war and witnessing the city like Dresden, heart of art and architecture, ruining and dying. Billy, throughout the plot leads his life on an Isthmus, accepting the horrible realities of Earthlings and then traversing into another land. The sense of timelessness and nothingness is adequately absorbed by the characters as well as by the plot which is also one of the key features of postmodern narrative elements. The narrative as well as the memory of war by Billy Pilgrim moves back and forth which lessens the pessimist dramatic effect of war and provides enough space for meaninglessness. Billy escapes death innumerable times, avoids talking about death, avoids sympathising with dead bodies, gives raw and crude description, yet there is death in almost every narrative thread that he weaves. The dichotomy between free will and predestination is represented by many biblical examples; the prayer posted on Billy's wall says:

> God Grant Me
> The Serenity To Accept
> The Things I Can Not Change,
> Courage
> To Change The Things I Can,
> And Wisdom To Tell The Difference (Vonnegut 50).

Contrastingly, Billy is also the representative of all Earthlings who have no control over their past, present or future. Travelling in time was not even Billy's own decision but predestined, "the time would not pass. Somebody was playing with the clocks, and not only with the electric clocks, but the wind-up kind too. The second hand on my watch would twitch once, and a year would pass, and then it would twitch again. There was nothing I could do about it" (Vonnegut 17).

Linda Hutcheon in her seminal work, *A Poetics of Postmodernism* observes that "the multiple and complex echoing points to the different possible functions of intertextuality... can both thematically and formally reinforce the text's message" (138). The assertiveness of trauma that came after war, meaninglessness of death and life, repetition of death events throughout the text can be read through the intertextual labyrinth that the author builds throughout. *Slaughterhouse Five* adopts two narrative styles. First, where Vonnegut is the omniscient narrator and he directly tries to build some sense of what he is going to do with the book. He searches for an appropriate form for his book which might give some sense to the dreadful experience of war of which he himself is a survivor. And the second where the narrator is Billy pilgrim, who is also an American prisoner of World War II, and he tries to find some sense and invents a fictional world of aliens which is the world where one can find hope and some order. Vonnegut's work is abundant with intertextual references on which Charles B. Harris comments by saying that it is a potpourri of "'Low fiction', 'criticism', 'documentary studies', 'high level realistic fiction', 'poetry', 'science fiction', – one could add light opera (The Pirates of Penzance), movie scripts, prayers, hymns, professional journals, newspaper, The Bible, drama, classical odes, dirty limericks, past popular songs, ('That old Gang of mine') ('Even Cent Cotton'), speeches, political propaganda (Campbell's Memo graph), pornographic magazines, forwards to books, Six Kilgore Trout novels and references to various writers of various ages and genres (Blake, Goethe, Schaherazade, Darwin)" (Hinchcliffe 185).

Vonnegut finds it very compulsive to toss his memory to envisage about war and its experience again because he has that endeavour to complete a book about Dresden bombing yet at the same time the idea of writing about Dresden bombing itself is very repulsive, uncomfortable and useless. He exhibits this by presenting a limerick:

> There was a young man from Stamboul,
> Who soliloquised thus to his tool;
> You took all my wealth
> And you ruined my health,
> And now you won't pee, you old fool. (2)

The limericks suggest the over use or over exhaustion of Vonnegut's memory which has resulted in some kind of artistic deficiency and points out to his deference to complete the book. T.J Matheson interprets this limerick as something which hints at penile dysfunction or impotency. He writes, "in the very irrelevance of the memory recalled, Vonnegut is making a subtle point about the fallibility of the human memory and its inability to retain a sense of perspective or stay on subjects of great importance for any length of time" (231). War and its after effects on its subjects have prevailed a barren feeling where there is no hope left. The author uses another song to suggest the circularity and absurdity of human life:

> My name is Yon Yonson,
> I work in Wisconsin,
> I work in a lumbermill there.
> The people I meet when I walk down the street,

They say, "what's your name?'
And I say,
My name is Yon Yonson
I work in Wisconsin… (3)

The song hints at the thematic circularity, repetition and narrative self-referentiality of a nursery rhyme which serves as a model for repeating narrative of the book. This song also reminds one of the poems by W.H Auden, "The Unknown Citizen", where the citizen who is known by his name and his occupation, keeps on repeating this so as to suggest that this is the only legitimate identity to live by. Jacques Derrida prophesises that "every text participates in one or several genres, there is no genre less text" (212). Vonnegut deliberately refers to 'The Children's Crusade' which his old friend O'Hare looks into the book written by Charles Mackay, *Extraordinary Popular Delusions and the Madness of Crowds,* published in 1841. They wanted to collect information on what the Children's Crusade is, which Vonnegut promises to write about O'Hare wife, Mary. Mackey, in his book, mentions about the Crusaders that, "the Crusaders were ignorant and savage men, that their motives were those of bigotry unmitigated, and that their pathway was one of blood and tears" (Vonnegut 13). This intertextual reference points at the absolute fascism that was being practised in Germany over that period. In order to reply back to German Crusade, the British Royal Air Force and United States Army Air Forces dropped explosive bombs on the Dresden city, which was the transportation centre of Nazi Germany. Mackney's book talks about the Children Crusade that started in 1213, where most of the innocent beings, unaware of the circumstances, were sold as slaves. Billy likewise participates in war and eventually becomes a prisoner without knowing beforehand the cost of war. O'Hare has another history book about Dresden which is titled, *Dresden, History, Stage and Gallery,* published in 1908. The book marks the evolution of Dresden as a city rich in art, culture and architecture, and how it expanded beautifully despite several destructions. The author of the book says, 'The devastation of the Dresden was boundless' which itself hints at the predetermination and future of the novel.

The dominant theme of predestination and no free will is asserted by the books that Vonnegut chooses to read on his journey. The first song from the book is "Words for the Wind", by Theodore Roethke and the lyrics are:

I wake to sleep, and take my waking slow.
I feel my fate in what I cannot fear.
I learn by going where I have to go. (Vonnegut 17)

The poem comments on the unknowable which is Tralfmadore land, which itself is invention of Billy Pilgrim. He learns on the foreign planet that there can be no wars and life can be happy too. He cannot avoid this revelation also as it is predetermined like the war and Dresden bombing. Here waking and sleeping is compared to life and death in which death is the ultimate destination. As much as these lines make sense for Vonnegut, it seems to contrast with what Billy Pilgrim has learned on Tralfmadore. The beings on the other planet believe in simultaneity of a moment. We can die at a moment while in other moments of life we live. *Celine and His Vision* by Erika Ostrovsky is another book which asserts the ever-pervading nature of death and nihilism. Celine was a French soldier in World War 1, who experienced hallucinations, and sleeplessness as after effects of War. He says, 'The truth is death, I have fought nicely against it as long as I could… danced with it, festooned it, waltzed it around… decorated it with streamers, titillated it…' (Vonnegut 17). Celine was obsessed with death and had learnt the ultimate truth. In one of the scenes of his book he wants everybody to freeze, to cease the moment, to avoid deaths but everything is determined beforehand and there is no free will.

The intertextual references used by the author help in shaping the book as a novel, he looks for history, how war soldiers dealt with death and the after effects of the war, how history has treated this pompous epic topic and how the general public has received it. He playfully hints at the horrors of war by using nursery rhymes and short limericks. Linda Hutcheon in her essay, "Historiographic Metafiction: Parody and the Intertextuality of History", confirms this by arguing that, "What we tend to call Postmodernism in literature today is usually characterised by intense self-reflexivity and overtly parodic inter-textuality" (3). The reference that Kurt Vonnegut draws parodies the grand narrative and provides ample space for Billy to escape the dark realities. Roland Weary thinks highly of himself as the saviour of Billy Pilgrim. He does so not out of love or altruism but he believes himself to be a catalyst to carry upon God's will and thinks that he is a real war hero. *The ThreeMuskeeters* is a novel by Alxandre Dumas in 1844, in which the three main characters, namely, Athos, Aramis, Porthos and D'Artagnan resemble the main characters of *Slaughterhouse Five*. Roland Weary acts as Athos who seems to be a father figure to D'Artagnan, which is Billy. In contrast to the pseudo chivalric Weary, Billy is represented as a cowardly hero, who could not even get a chance to show his courage. Vonnegut's draws his comparison to the hero of the novel, *The Red Badge of Courage* by Stephen Crane. Although Crane like Vonnegut has never experienced war first hand, his work, however, is known for its realistic portrayal of war. The protagonist of Crane's novel endures internal as well as external battle and the effects of war which crane has termed as, 'psychological portrayal of fear'.

EliotRosewater, who is Billy's partner in mental hospital introduces Billy to some of the good books that he holds onto till end. One of the books mentioned by him is Feodor Dostoevsky's *The Brothers Karamazov.* Rosewater mentions "everything there was to know about life was in *The Brothers Karamazov* by Feodor Dostoevsky" (Vonnegut 83). He directly hints at the question of free will which is addressed by the Russian author. The author accepts that every individual has free will and can practice it and even recommends it as compulsory exercise with regards to spiritual pursuits. Vonnegut puts it contrarily rather ironically that everything is predestined, there is no such thing as free will and Billy lives by this belief his whole life. Roland Barthes argues that text is a "multidimensional space in which a variety of writings, none of them original, blend and clash" (146). Vonnegut refers to several authors and history books in his work but one significantly drawn character and reference is Kilgore Trout who is said to be Vonnegut himself or a caricature of him. He claims to have read most of Trout's book but makes explicit reference to only six which are: *The Big Board, Maniacs in the Fourth Dimensión, The Guiless Wonder, The Gospel from Outer Space, Jesús and the Time Machine* and The *Money Tree.* There is a stark similarity in the personal as well as professional lives of the two authors. Vonnegut earned a living by working in public relations before the success of *Slaughter House Five* while Trout used to work "as a circulation man for the Ilium Gazette, manage newspaper delivery boys, bullies and flatters and cheats little kids" (Vonnegut 136). Kilgore Trout is unknown to the world as a writer even if he has written plenty of books on Science fiction. Only Eliot Rosewater is the one who has heard of him and mentions about him to Billy. Trout himself comments that, "He did not think of himself as a writer for the simple reason that the world had never allowed him to think of himself in this way" (Vonnegut 138). Eliot Rosewater and Billy Pilgrim are roommates in psychiatry hospitals for veterans, where both of them are trying to recover from the dreadful impact of war. To their rescue they turn to science fiction of Kilgore Trout 'to re-invent themselves and their universe'.

The Big Board by Trout tells the experience of two human beings, earthling man and a woman who were kidnapped by extra-terrestrials who were put on a display in a zoo on a planet called Zircon 212. The novel provides the baseline to Billy Pilgrim to invent an alien planet Tralfmadore and the incidents almost resemble. The meaninglessness of life in fantasy as well as in realistic 'fantasy' life of Billy has been asserted by the reference. He is also kidnapped by the aliens in order to perform for the crowd at zoo. Another novel which insinuates the absurd attachment which human beings have developed with capital and gathering money is *The Money Tree,* which alludes to the futuristic capital system that is going to haunt and take over humanity "it had twenty-dollars bills for leaves. Its flowers were government bonds. Its fruits were diamonds. It attracted human beings who killed each other around the roots and made very good fertilizer" (Vonnegut 137). Ironical use of human being as things which help the capital grow tells us about the height of capitalism in that time when the novel was published. *The Maniacs in the Fourth Dimension*, directly hints at the anxiety and suffering which Billy and Eliot Rosewater go through after the war. Nobody in their family is able to accept or understand the mental illness which is real suffering for them. Vonnegut alludes to this work ironically and satirises the comic demonstration of little knowledge of human beings. *The Gutless Wonder,* "it was about a robot who had bad breath, who became popular after his halitosis was cured" (Vonnegut 137). Ironically the people who bombed Dresden are compared to the robot who looked like human beings and dropped burning jellied gasoline on 'real' human beings. Trout gives us the justification for this act by saying, they did it so because, "they had no conscience, and no circuits, which would allow them to imagine what was happening to the people on the ground" (Vonnegut 138). The reference used by Vonnegut satirises American's dehumanising dealing with Dresden and its people. The Robot was accepted by his people only after he got himself cured of his bad breath, however, they had no objection to the dreadful crime he commits. *The Gospel from Outer Space* is about an alien who comes from an outer space like Tralfmadore, and takes upon studying Christianity in order to know why Christians are so cruel. He concludes that Christ, who doesn't look so is the son of "most powerful being in the universe" (Vonnegut 89). He thought that the main content of the Gospel must be to develop compassion and kindness instead it taught "Before you kill somebody make absolutely sure that he isn't well connected" (Vonnegut 89).So, the other being from outer space gifted a new gospel which claims Jesus to be "Nobody" having "no influence" (Vonnegut 89). Vonnegut associated Billy Pilgrim with Jesus Christ consciously and often draws references from hymns and gospels. These lines from Christmas Carol compare Jesus and Billy by saying:

> The cattle are lowing,
> The Baby awakes.
> But the little Lord Jesus
> No crying He makes. (Vonnegut 162).

Throughout the war or even after surviving as a prisoner of war and having seen so many deaths Billy Pilgrim does not shed a tear. He doesn't prove himself to be a true Christian by showing compassion towards those who do not survive the war or who were killed brutally. The cruelty of war and the destruction has made him emotionally barren and desensitised that he is unable to respond to death in a humanising way. Vonnegut like Billy defers the descriptions of death scenes and causalities by writing "so it goes...". *Jesus and the Time Machine,* is a book in which a time traveller inquires and proves that death of Jesus Christ was a real incident. His claim includes that Jesus was "five feet and three and a half inches" and he was really dead after his crucifixion" (Vonnegut 168). This established more humanly connections between Jesus and Billy Pilgrim. Most of the Kilgore Trout's stories provide counterpoints as well as points of intersection what Billy had believed in. Julia Kristeva theorises that, "any text is constructed as a mosaic of quotations; any text is the absorption and transformation of another" (66). The Science fiction stories provided by Trout give ample space to incorporate and justify the dehumanising effects of war and escapism from the effect of it.

The book is abundant with pastiche narrative elements incorporating metafiction, magic realism, temporal distortion all of these combining together to make it a work written about the horrific incident of Dresden Bombing. "The term Postmodernism, when used in fiction, should by analogy, best be reserved to describe fiction that is at once metafictional and historical in its echoes of the texts and contexts of the past" (Hutcheon 3). The authorial presence significant in the opening chapter directly conveys what it takes to write a historical account of actual events though Vonnegut has "changed all the names" because it is also a fictional account (1). This attempt of writing about Dresden destruction is an assertive fiction assimilating the real historical accounts of various writers which Vonnegut consciously mentions in the narrative. Billy meets Prof. Rumfoord who is working on one volume history of the Army Air Force in World War II which is condensed from a twenty-seven volume *Official History of the Army Air Force* in World War

II. David Irving's American edition of *The Destruction of Dresden* justifies the cruelty and loss done to Dresden on America's part and creates this meta narrative to make people believe how important it is to have wars. Air Marshal Saund by comments in the book, "That the bombing of Dresden was a great tragedy none can deny. That it was really a military necessity few, after reading this book will believe" (Vonnegut 154). The book is loaded with other historical references which are quite real and prove the authenticity of Billy's narrative. The description of Nazi concentration camps, The Civil War, Atomic Bombing of Hiroshima and the Battle of Dunkrik provide enough space and imagination to envisage the mass level destruction which is ironically human motivated. Vonnegut not only romanticises war rather provides the real, crude picture of war where there is no place for glamour, hero, enemy or drama. Billy Pilgrim who was deeply ingrained in the dark realities of human life, when returns finds it difficult to show compassion or emotionally attach himself with those who have been the victims of the tragedy.

Vonnegut himself plays a central character in the first and last chapter of the novel and marks his impressions of living that horrific reality throughout chapter two to nine. The opening lines mark that it is going to be a real and first-hand experience of war as he writes, "ALL THIS HAPPENED, more or less. The war parts, anyway, are pretty much true. One guy I knew really *was* shot in Dresden for taking a teapot that wasn't his. Another guy I knew really *did* threaten to have his personal enemies killed by hired gunmen after the war. And so on" (1). The way he formatively writes this sentence, the conscious use of capital letters to assert the fact that all that brutality really did take place and it is now a part of history, a past that is no longer there because it is not Billy's Tralfmadore but Vonnegut's exercise to put his haunting experience into something as concrete and everlasting as words. He declares the climax as soon as the first chapter starts, "I think the climax of the book will be the execution of poor old Edgar Derby" (2). Vonnegut's deliberate use of poioumena which according to Alastir Fowler is used to calculate to explore the thin line between fiction and reality. It makes it even more a rigorous exercise for reader and author to assimilate the truth. However, Billy's narrative is written in 'Telegraphic Schizophrenic manner' which incorporates science fiction as well as real incident of Dresden bomb attack because Billy was also present there. He is unable to mark the difference between real world that he lives in and the temporal space of Tralfmadore land which is simultaneous and everlasting. Vonnegut makes it in 'Telegraphic Schizophrenic' manner because of Billy's time travel. The non-linear narrative and scattered chronology make the reader actively jump into the plot where it is a task on the reader's part to join the jots and make sense of the meaningless and absurd situation. Billy's psychological condition is echoed by the scattered chronology because he has started living Tralfmadore's reality where, "The Tralfmadorians can look at all the different moments just the way we can look at a stretch of the Rocky Mountains, for instance. They can see how permanent all the mountains are, and they can look at any moment that interests them. It is just an illusion we have here on Earth that one moment follows another one, like beads on a string" (Vonnegut 22).

The fragmented grand narrative and portrayal of war in fragments, dispersal of events of Dresden bombing or even the chronological events of the life of Billy Pilgrim give Vonnegut a sense of escapism and another plot mending into the grand narrative of war invites reader to make any meaning of all that has happened and is happening in the life of Billy Pilgrim. He as a character of the novel does not evolve organically rather, we know at first that Billy is a time traveller but Vonnegut hides the actual cause what has made him to do so. All the dispersal and fragmented series of epic events represent the chaotic universe. Billy's character is also fragmented as he is part of two worlds, one which is nihilistic and other the Tralfmadorian land where there can be possibility of some negotiations, some meaning. Vonnegut deliberately tries to avoids everything which is heavy and traumatising but the work he has to endure till last demands encounter with real truth which is war and destruction. Repetition of 'so it goes…' and 'Poo-tee-weet' by bird reflects that there is nothing intelligible which Vonnegut or Billy pilgrim has to say about war. The later phrase has no meaning and so does war; rather, it is repeated again and again to find some hope and meaning if there is any.

Conclusion

Slaughter House Five proves to be a postmodernist work which departs itself from structured and ordered modern labyrinths of narratives. Through the narrative style which aligns itself with the horrific event of Dresden bombing and life of Billy Pilgrim, Vonnegut questions the linear history and linear narrative. The plot lies somewhere between history and metafiction which disrupts the clear boundaries between the fantasy and reality. Both the narratives work on their own trajectory and abrupt jumping back and forth flow gives the complete sense of meaninglessness. *Slaughter House Five* can be perceived as another literary work that feeds upon and contributes to the actual event of bombing and exposes the brutal external as well as internal consequences of Second World War. The play between narrator and author brings the work on another level which exploits all the dimensions of postmodernist narrative and subverts the modern narrative techniques.

Works Cited

Barthes, Roland. "The Death of the Author." *Image, Music, Text,* Fontana Press, 1977, pp. 142-48.

Derrida, Jacques and A. Ronell. "The Law of Genre." *Critical Inquiry*, vol. 7, no. 1, 1980, pp. 55-81. *JSTOR*, www.jstor.org/stable/1343176.

Edelstein, Arnold. *Slaughter House Five: Time Out of Joint.* Johns Hopkins University Press, vol. 1, no. 2, 1974, pp. 128-39. *JSTOR*, www.jstor.org/ stable/25111023.

Harris B., Charles. "TIME, UNCERTAINITY AND KURT VONNEGUT, JR.: A READING OF "SLAUGHTER HOUSE FIVE." *The Centennial Review*, vol. 30, no. 3, 1976, pp. 228-43, *JSTOR*, www.jstor.org/stable/23738361.

Hinchcliffe, Richard. ""Would'st Thou Be in a Dream": John Bunyan's *The Pilgrim's Progress* and Kurt Vonnegut's *Slaughterhouse-Five.*" *European Journal of American Culture*, vol. 20, no. 3, November 2002, pp. 183-96. *Research Gate*, doi:10.1386/ejac.20.3.183.

Hutcheon, Linda. *A Poetics of Postmodernism.* Routledge, 1998.

---. "Historiographic Metafiction: Parody and Intertextuality of History." *Intertextuality and Contemporary American Fiction.* Johns Hopkins UP, 1989.

Kristeva, Julia. *Desire in Language: A Semiotic Approach to Literature and Art.* Columbia UP, 1980.

Vonnegut Kurt. *Slaughterhouse Five.* Vintage, 2000.

Waugh, Patricia. *Metafiction: The Theory and Practice of Self-Conscious Fiction.* Methuen, 1984.

CHAPTER 3

Judaism and American Culture Interface: Family as a Metanarrative in Bernard Malamud's *The Fixer*

Anju Jagpal and *Pooja Goyal*

Bernard Malamud's *The Fixer* (1966) can be taken as a postmodernist novel that it challenges the metanarrative of marriage based on traditional, religious and social norms as well as patriarchy. In the novel, *The Fixer*, it is shown that the major reason behind the collapse of marital ties lies in the inability of both spouses to give understanding, accommodation, tolerance and empathy. In Malamud's novels, Quart finds:

> In comparison, women, human relationships generally, are peripheral concerns. Malamud's heroes usually live alone and are usually bachelors, although occasionally a man's wife is temporarily away, or recently divorced from him. The old Jews have mournful, faceless help mates: the younger men occasionally make a special living arrangement with a woman, but Malamud rarely shows us a man and a woman genuinely sharing a place and a life, not to mention a family. (140)

In the beginning of the novel, the protagonist, though a self-styled free thinker, is actually a demanding Jewish husband who adds to the woes of his wife by avoiding her because of her inability to produce a child. Earlier, Yakov, in his courtship of Raisl, visited her home frequently, shared food with her and her father and helped them in renovating their hut. Only at an impulse, Raisl and Yakov indulged in love making and Raisl, being a Jew, felt guilt at succumbing to desire and sex without social and religious sanction. They married but a hiatus appeared between them after the sixth year of their marriage. Gradually, it becomes clear that Shmuel's approval of Yakov was the root cause which prompted Raisl into marriage, not her own love for him. Yakov relates, "Besides that, your father was behind me, pushing with both hands. If I married you, the world would change... everyday a rainbow" (*The Fixer* 285). However, Raisl views differently from her father and she also seems not in love with Yakov, "You [Yakov] can believe me I was afraid to marry you, but you were affectionate then, and when a person is lonely it's easy to lean toward a tender word" (*The Fixer* 285).

Raisl rejects Yakov's idea that a woman's primary function in marriage is to conceive and serve children. She rejects altogether the submissive status which is usually attributed to women in Jewish homes. She does not believe in the old marriage code, accepting Yakov's patriarchal attitude. Raisl's extra marital affair and her elopement with a musician of the village inn show not only her feminist identity but also her reaction towards Jewish assumption of taking woman only as a physical comfort to men.

The warm relationships in Yakov's small family undergo a lot of stress and strain. Yakov also finds his loving father-in-law somewhat rude towards him. When Shmuel assertively favours his daughter, Yakov does not like him and affirms, "A father-in-law's blood was [is] thicker than water" (*The Fixer* 10). Instead Yakov "feels warmth for Shmuel his father-in-law and cries at his death, even though Shmuel had saddled Yakov with his undowered 'false' daughter and a hopeless horse and cart" (Quart 143). Shmuel says, "She sinned but she was desperate" (*The Fixer* 8). On the one hand, he objects Yakov, "... did you stop sleeping with her for months? Is that a way to treat a wife?" (*The Fixer* 6). On the other, Shmuel defends Raisl by saying, "... my daughter wanted to run away from here [Tsarist Russia and shtetl as unsafe for Jews] but you wouldn't go" (*The Fixer* 11). Moreover, it becomes too late for Yakov to realise the worth of Raisl's words after reading a pamphlet about the decision of previous Russian Tsar Nicholas I for starting pogrom against Russian Jews. No doubt Yakov becomes a *schlemiel*, a lonesome and humiliated fellow calling Raisl a whore as he says, "I fix what's broken – except in the heart" (*The Fixer* 7). However, he does not lose his heart and begins anew.

Yakov finds out, "... what suffering has taught me is the uselessness of suffering" (*The Fixer* 333). He starts again to fix the broken pieces of his life, accepts the adverse situation and does not bother much about Raisl's departure from his home. He says, "... who's interested [in Raisl]... Five years going on six is enough of patience. I've had enough. I might have waited the legal ten. But she danced off with some dirty stranger, so I've had my fill, thanks" (*The Fixer* 10-11). Yakov is no more interested in living in the village as he says, "It moulders and the Jews moulder in it. Here we're all prisoners" (*The Fixer* 11). He remarks:

> He was leaving because he had earned a worse living... he was a childless husband – 'alive but dead' the Talmud described such a man – as well as embittered, deserted one. Yet she had been faithful he would have stayed. Then better she hadn't been. He should be grateful to the fruitless life. (*The Fixer* 20)

Yakov's personal life goes into a spin as priorities change in his life: he chooses a "job that pays rubles not noodles" (*The Fixer* 12) over his wife or family. He further says, "I'd sell my last shirt to be a millionaire. Maybe, by luck, I'll make my fortune in the outside world (*The Fixer* 12). The shaving of his beard, his departure to "Holy Kiev, mother of Russian cities" (*The Fixer* 20) and his wish to head for Amsterdam and then to America (*The Fixer* 13) with his fixing tools of "carpentering, painting and roofing" (*The Fixer* 37) and philosophical books shows his strong will to start a life anew. The narrator remarks, "He dreamed of good fortune, accomplishment, affluence, He had a comfortable home, good business – may be a small factory of some kind – a faithful wife, dark-haired, pretty, and three healthy children, God bless them" (*The Fixer* 24).

Yakov tries to lay the foundation of his new home as "a free thinker" (*The Fixer* 86) – independent of traditions, authority or established religious beliefs. He chooses to be a rationalist who would end his sufferings without being a follower of *The Talmud* or *The Bible*. Leslie Field rightly says:

> He [Malamud] is a brother to the many intellectual and literary Jews who years ago left the *shtetl* and traditional Judaism to reach out into the world. They rejected the confines of the past.... In so doing they as people and the characters they gave us all took on the qualities of marginality as these writers ignored, skirted, homogenised, or rejected important concerns of the Jewish people. (114)

Yakov assumes new surname of Ivanovitch Dologushev, though it seems hanging "on him like a suit of stolen clothes" (*The Fixer* 112). No doubt Yakov is fearsome because of his stamp of Jewishness as "a born Jew can't hide the Zhid in his face. This [Yakov] is a foxy bastard" (*The Fixer* 112). However, he proves himself "a man who decides for himself if he wants to believe in religion. May be an agonistic also" (*The Fixer* 87). He goes to see an orthodox Church, Larvae catacombs and the hand of Saint Andrew there, but joins neither any of the religious sects nor follows Judaism. This shows that "in each novel the decision for change is gradually revealed to the consciousness of the hero as the beginning of a quest, not merely for a new life in a new environment, but for a new free self" (Handy 82). That is why Yakov does not take the warnings of the boatsman seriously who says, "... the time's not far off when... our Lord [Jesus Christ], who they [Jewish] crucified, wants his right *The Fixerul* revenge" (*The Fixer* 28). In his passion of a new rich life, Yakov does not bother about adverse political and religious scenes in Kiev, "a city of strangers – in a sense a forbidden place" (*The Fixer* 20), "full of churches and anti-Semites" (*The Fixer* 11) and where the wealthy Jews and the professional classes only can get residence certificates. It seems that Yakov wishes to prove his worth to Raisl, Shmuel and the whole village by establishing himself in Kiev where lies the dangerous Kiev Union of Russian People, Society of the Black Hundreds and Double Eagle and also Nicholas II, the last Russian Tsar whose combined slogan is: SAVE RUSSIA FROM THE JEWS (*The Fixer* 4). They kill Jews in no time as they say "it's good for business" (*The Fixer* 309).

In Kiev, Yakov seems to be jumping out of frying pan into fire. He comes to have a happy and rich home, but gets a prison house. The company of Zinaida Nikolaevna (Zina), the crippled daughter of Nikolai Maximovitch Lebedev living in the Plossky district raises new hopes in Yakov when she says, "Come, Yakov Ivanovitch, there's more to life than work" (*The Fixer* 48). It seems that the crippled Zina is not able to find a life partner and when she meets the needy Yakov, she does not wish to let him go. Yakov helps Nikolai who offers him to do some repair work into their flat for forty rubles and later a job as an overseer to their brickyard with a pay of forty-five rubles and a stay there. Yakov thinks, "A few months' experience at this kind of work and other opportunities might [may] open for him" (*The Fixer* 48). However, in the brickyard, his enmity with the workers Proshko, Richter and Serdiuk who he catches red handed pilfering bricks there, raises the wind against him (58). They become the major witness of the incident when Yakov helps injured Hasid. They find Yakov a Jew and accuse him of a ritual murder of a twelve year old Christian boy, Zhenia Golov. Moreover, Proshko and his company burn down the stable of Yakov at the brickyard, making the dreams of Yakov's happy home with Zina collapse. His counterfeit identification papers are discovered and he is arrested in the name of His Majesty Nicholas II by thirty police officials with their drawn pistols and swords along with two representatives of the Office of the Chief Prosecuting Attorney of the District Superior Court (*The Fixer* 69).

Malamud, as a postmodernist, shows that the religious orthodoxy is responsible for the destruction of mankind on one hand and erosion of human as also conjugal relationships on the other because love for each other is not the base of human life. Yakov stands where he started having same experiences of broken relations with Zina like those of Raisl. Zina who shares dinner with Yakov, uses high sounding words like "a man of sobriety and sound sense" (*The Fixer* 46) for him, finds him an extraordinary labourer (*The Fixer* 43), shows too much concern for his clothes, work and staying place and desperately wants sex with him even at the time of her menstruation (*The Fixer* 53) shows that she is yet another chameleon like the others. Zina along with her father Nikolai who shows himself "a miserable man, melancholic, a heavy drinker" (*The Fixer* 39), sensitive enough to cry over "the Sermon on the Mount" (*The Fixer* 38) and sent congratulatory letters to Yakov on his achievement in brickyard, now, both turn out to be anti-Semites. They write two letters each against Yakov castigating him as a fraudulent Jew. Zina backs out from her words for Yakov:

> I can only say I was on the whole uncomfortable in his presence, although of course truly grateful that he had assisted Papa that time he slipped in the snow. Afterwards I detested him because he tried to assault me [sexually]. I told him firmly I never wished to see him again.... I saw he was cut in the manner of Jewish males. I could not help seeing. (*The Fixer* 90-91)

Yakov has already known it if he "said 'Jew' aloud, she'd run in six directions" (45). However, he admits, "I was a fool to agree to go to her room in the first place. I should have gone home the minute I finished my work and not been tempted by a table full of all kinds of food" (93).

Thomas Docherty's statement that postmodern narrative "enacts the character as *Dasein*, the character who constantly escapes the fixity of identity... whereby the assumed or desired totality of a real self is endlessly 'dispositioned', always a 'being there', as opposed to a being here, a being present to itself" (144) can be seen in the character of Yakov. Yakov appears to be a patriarch seen in his dominating attitude with Raisl, however, at the same time he emerges as a new man in the postmodernist sense who finds Judaism suffocating and as the cause of his grief. In previous realistic novels related to holocaust or torture done to Jews, the Jewish authors try to raise their voice getting sympathy for the Jews, however, in *The Fixer*, the protagonist tries to make a distance from Jewish history and traditions. He finds, "... for a Jew it was the same wherever he went – he carried a remembered pack on his back – a condition of servitude, diminished opportunity, vulnerability" (*The Fixer*

255). He begins to "curse history, anti-Semitism, fate, and even, occasionally the Jews" (*The Fixer* 155) because being a Jew, he finds his dreams of loving home broken on one side and himself entangled in a criminal case on the other. He asserts, "What was being a Jew but an everlasting curse? He was sick of their history, destiny, blood guilt" (*The Fixer* 227). The world avenges them because as Grubeshov says, "The Jews dominated the world and we feel ourselves under their yoke" (*The Fixer* 226). Yakov opines, "There was no 'reason,' there was only their plot against a Jew, any Jew; he was the accidental choice for the sacrifice... being born a Jew meant being vulnerable to history, including its worst errors" (*The Fixer* 155).

Moreover, it is important to mention here that Yakov finds the passage of the Gospel of John in *Old Testament* the façade of bloodshed between Jews and gentiles. He reads, "Unless you eat the flesh of the Son of man and drink His blood, you have no life in you; he who eats My flesh and drinks My blood has eternal life, and I will raise him up on the last day" (*The Fixer* 233). The anti-Semites partake the flesh and blood of their children rather than bread and wine as also use the words as a political propaganda against Jews. It is also important to mention here that it is his helplessness that he calls for a "Jewish journalist" and "sincere philanthropist" (*The Fixer* 161) in the name of religious fraternity to set himself free, but no Jew comes.

Another remarkable feature seen in the novel is the indoctrination of high values and rules of society in children by the parents. Malamud shows that the innocent children become prey to the unscrupulous parents at home and the innocent beings like Yakov that of the scandalous political-religious society. The demonic mother of Zheniz Golov, Marfa Vladimirovna Golov's sexual affair with Stepen Bulkin becomes a reason behind the murder of Zhenia on one side and arrest of Yakov on the other. Nobody can forget the words of Kogin the prison guard, "You plan one thing and get another. Life plays no favorites and what's the use of hoping for it? The children were ruined by their mother, a woman of unsettled character and lax ways" (*The Fixer* 271). Malamud calls her "a wicked woman, stupid yet cunning, with the morals of a hardened prostitute" (*The Fixer* 169). "Marfa and Raisl merge into a single phantom enticing Bok sexually to his destruction" (Quart 144). First, Marfa and Stepen coveted and spent a legacy of five hundred rubles of life insurance which Zhenia's father had left him. Marfa came out as a witch that blinded Stepan (for life with carbolic acid) who she loved more than anyone else in the world and

Stepan revenged himself on her by killing her son who was grossly neglected by her. The torn wallpaper, a dirty sheet and a torn blanket of Zhenia's room shows the cruelty and carelessness of Marfa. Moreover, it is said that Zhenia was murdered because firstly he had discovered Yakov's participation in criminal activities (*The Fixer* 281) "with a group of other Hebrews, suspected smugglers, house breakers and other criminal elements in the cellar of synagogue" (*The Fixer* 280). Secondly "he wished to enter the priesthood" (*The Fixer* 133), but his dream was destroyed. Moreover, Marfa threatens Sofya Shiskovsky, Marfa's neighbor who sees Zhenia's corpse in the bathtub at Marfa's place and Sofya along with her family moves to Moscow. Marfa does not show any repentance rather shows herself in good light and tries to gain sympathy from others by saying:

> I'm a widow of stainless character, pure and simple. My husband, who was a telegrapher, deserted me... later died of consumption, which served him right for the way he mistreated us. I support myself by hard work and that's why my house that you're in isn't the neatest, but my child has always had a roof over his head, and my life has been one of irreproachable toil (*The Fixer* 120).

Even the authorities accept her as a "martyred mother of a martyred child" (*The Fixer* 118) and declares that Marfa's composed behaviour at her son's funeral was the 'behavior of a dignified person in control of her sentiments although involved in a profound personal loss... guilt is not a matter of facial expression but of evidence. Marfa even emotionally blackmails Yakov by writing a letter to him in which she says:

> In God's name give an ear to a mother's pleas. I am worn out by the wicked insults and insinuations that have been wrongfully cast on myself by certain worthless people – including certain neighbors I have cut myself off from, without any proof whatsoever (*The Fixer* 243).

Yakov is so shocked to see her overconfident and dramatic behaviour that he ironically observes, "Lying naked on the fixer's mattress, her legs spread apart, she [Marfa] promised many goyish delights if Yakov would [will] confess to the priest at the peephole" (*The Fixer* 248).

The binary oppositions play a part in the novel and give the novel a postmodernist touch: parents/demons, home/prison, place of living/place of politics, progress/exploitation, etc. are some of the points that simulate the relations in a family of today. Yakov finds that there is a hidden reality behind what meets the eye of a first glance and he says, "Behind the world lies another world" (*The Fixer* 171). The Tsar

Nicholas II projects his image as "the most sensitive" creature (*The Fixer* 221) which he is really not. He shows that his love for his son who is suffering from hemophilia makes it difficult for him to forgive Yakov for his crime against Zhenia. Yakov challenges the Tsar for his crocodile tears, "You say you are kind and prove it with pogroms" (*The Fixer* 334). Yakov feels, "He had fished for a herring and had been snatched by a shark" (*The Fixer* 155). On one hand, Marfa needs a person to put the suspicion of her murdered son on, the Tsar too needs a distraction to keep the people from revolting against his crimes (*The Fixer* 227) and Grubeshov, Colonel Bodyansky and the Deputy Warden who all want to get promoted by impressing the Tsar, all get Yakov Bok as a scapegoat "to save their own necks" (*The Fixer* 170). In other words, ironical enough, Yakov is "chosen to murder the corpse" (*The Fixer* 315). Moreover, Grubeshov informs Yakov, "We want you sentenced to a severe life imprisonment as a lesson for all to see of Jewish perfidy" (*The Fixer* 200).

Even then Yakov says, "The truth is that things are bad though how bad I don't know myself. The case is clear enough – it's a bad joke from top to bottom – but it's fixed up in the worst way with the political situation" (*The Fixer* 305). Yakov who says, "Politics is not in my nature" (*The Fixer* 45), becomes a victim of political unreliability" (*The Fixer* 62). Under the orders of Tsar, the authorities keep him in a large cell under the Plossky District Courthouse crowded with twenty-five hard core criminals and then in strict solitary confinement. He sleeps on a hard wooden platform, lives with mosquitoes and bugs and also suffers humiliating six body searches per day. He is given soup (shared by other prisoners too) from the buckets containing dead mice and cockroaches. He has to fight for his food, the slow poison, with which he suffers from diarrhea and fever. The sores of his feet are mercilessly cut and treated with carbolic acid without anesthesia. His knees and hands are bandaged with garbage rags. He is "imprisoned, starved, chained like an animal to a wall although he was innocent" (*The Fixer* 315). Berezhinsky, a Police personnel, pours urine on his head and he faces hateful stares of Russian people and false statements of another prisoner Gronfein as a witness. Even the gentiles Bibikov the lawyer, Kogin the guard and Fetyukov the prisoner who have been in Yakov's favour are also shot on the charges of insubordination to the Tsar. Yakov becomes helpless to think, "What is it Spinoza says? If the state acts in ways that are abhorrent to human nature it's the lesser evil to destroy it. Death to the anti-Semites!" (*The Fixer* 335). According to him, anti-Semites include not Christians but the dictators who can kill both gentiles and Jews for their interests. "In fact his Jew may become indistinguishable from the non-Jew as he becomes homogenised in a larger, non-Jewish world" (Field 109). He may emerge as everyman – a prey of the authorities.

Yakov, in a way, finds himself caught in the net of a difficult situation in which he is brutally treated by his family on one hand and authoritative politicians and the men of God including rabbis and priests add on his sorrows and sufferings on the other. Yakov constantly blames Raisl for whatever wrong happens to him. He says, "She ran off with an unknown party and that's why I'm in jail now. If she hadn't done that I would have stayed where I belonged, which means where I was born" (*The Fixer* 74).

To take Yakov-Raisl relationship, Malamud seems to satirize the traditional concept of marriage. In the prison, Yakov sings a tale of Hosea and Gomer from the Hebrew Bible in which it is stated that on the orders of God, Hosea has to marry Gomer, an unfaithful woman, however she leaves him for another man. Hosea sings:

> I will hedge up thy way with thorns,
> I will make a wall against her,
> That she will not find her paths...
> And she shall seek them, but shall not find them;
> Then she will say: I will go and return to my first husband. (*The Fixer* 242)

Hosea redeems her and brings her back to home. However, in the novel, Yakov neither brings Raisl back nor he desires to do so.

The Fixer can be taken into the category of 'Historiographic Metafiction,' a term given by Linda Hutcheon, a postmodernist who says that "Historiographic Metafiction represents a challenging of the (related) conventional forms of fiction and history through its acknowledgement of their inescapable [parodic] textuality" (11). The novel parodies not only Job, the noble but impractical character in the Hebrew Bible, but it also parodies the Bible, the old religion of Judaism and old family norms. Foer seems partially right when he says, "As the charges against him grow and deform, Yakov becomes a Job-like figure" (*The Fixer* x). However, the character of Yakov parodies Job's sacrifice of his family and his belongings for the will of God. Job, in *The Hebrew Bible,* is presented as a prosperous family man who has a firm faith in God but God takes away all his holdings including his health, offspring and property. Later, God rewards his obedience and subservience by restoring his health, doubling his original wealth, giving him seven new sons and three new daughters and a long life of 140 years thereafter. As against it, Yakov says, "To win a lousy bet with the devil he [God] killed off all the servants and innocent children of Job. For that alone I hate him.... Job is an invention and so is God" (*The Fixer* 258). In the novel, no (Judaic or Christian) god comes to end Yakov's sufferings. When Raisl leaves him, he curses God in the words:

> A meshummed [A Jew's conversion into a Christian or a traitor who cut off from family, friends and Israel] gives up one God for another. I don't want either. We live in a world where the clock ticks fast while he's [God] on his timeless mountain staring in space. He doesn't see us and he doesn't care. Today I want my piece of bread, not in paradise. (*The Fixer* 17)

Yakov remains imprisoned for more than two and a half years bearing torture. He cries out, "Mama-Papa, save me! Shmuel, Raisl-anybody save me!" (*The Fixer* 183). "He cried out of the deepest part of him, a narrow pit, but no one appeared or answered, or looked at him, neither friend nor stranger" (*The Fixer* 239). That is why he does not believe in the Jewish religiosity of Shmuel who views that the sufferings come to Yakov because he does not read *The Torah*. Shmuel says, "Don't look for God in the wrong place, look in the Torah, the law," (*The Fixer* 258). Yakov himself becomes sometimes doubtful: "God was punishing him for his unbelief". But at the same time he realises, "He was after all, the jealous God. 'Thou shalt worship no other Gods before me,' not even to Gods" (*The Fixer* 153).

Yakov also finds the lap of God as the spider's web from which he cannot come out. He seems to reject the metanarrative of the Bible and the Talmud and also the existence of God:

> Don't talk to me about God. I want no part of God. When you need him most he's farthest away. Enough is enough.... I blame him [God] for not existing. Or if he does it's on the moon or stars but not here. The thing is not to believe or the waiting becomes unbearable. I can't hear his voice and never have. I don't need him unless he appears. (*The Fixer* 256)

He sings the psalms ironically to make fun of the myth of existence of God. He sings:

> 'Arise, O Lord; O God, lift up Thy hand;
> Forget not the humble.'
> 'Break Thou the arm of the wicked'
> ...
> He thought of himself pursuing his enemies with God at his side, but when he looked at God all he saw or heard was a loud Ha Ha. (*The Fixer* 209)

The views of Benedictus de Spinoza (1632-1677), which Yakov firmly believes in, give authenticity to Yakov's disbelief in sacred God. He agrees with Spinoza's idea of *Deus sive Natura* (God equates nature) that challenges the authenticity of the Hebrew Bible and the nature of God in the Portuguese Jewish and gentile communities in Amsterdam and the Jewish authorities issued a *cherem* (order of ostracism) against Spinoza at the age of twenty three. Spinoza's statement in his work, *Short Treatise of God, Man, and His Well Being*, "Nature consists of infinite attributes, each of which is perfect in its kind. And this is just equivalent to the definition usually given of God" (*The Fixer* 42) directly challenges the concept of scriptural God who actively responds to events in the universe.

In the novel, Yakov never listens to the prescriptions of rabbis or priests – the men of God – as he says, "Let him [rabbi] stay out of my business and I'll stay out of his. All is all he's an ignorant man" (6). First, rabbis have spoiled his family life with Raisl as she ran behind these rabbis instead of consulting doctors for a cure for infidelity. Second, in Kiev, unfortunately, he happens to meet the priests who give horrified ritual turn to his case in the name of safety of Christian children and family. The priest to the Russians more often known as "charlatan" (*The Fixer* 172) makes the situation more complicated for him by declaring:

> Since the destruction of their Temple in Jerusalem by the legions of Titus there has been no sacrificial altar for animals in their synagogues, and it has come about, therefore, that the killing of gentiles, in particular innocent children, is accepted as a fitting substitute. Even their philosopher Maimonides, whose writings were suppressed in our country in 1844, orders Jews to murder Christian children. Did I not tell you they think of us as animals? (*The Fixer* 131).

Yakov's free thinking is given the name of "self-incriminating atheism"... "in order to hide from the legal authorities that he had committed a vile religious murder of a child for the sole and evil purpose of providing his Hasidic compatriots with the uncorrupted human blood needed to bake the Passover matzos and unleavened cakes in the synagogue" (*The Fixer* 297). Grubeshov falsely accuses Yakov as a member of Jewish revolutionary groups like of "Social Democrats, Socialist-Revolutionists, Jewish Bund, Zionist, Seymist or Volkspartei (*The Fixer* 97) and blood drinker Hasid Misnogid (*The Fixer* 99). The authorities keep his beard long and his hair cut in a manner making him look like *kosher* ["ritually pure Jew"]. To prove him that he is a confirmed Jew, a prayer shawl and phylacteries (very small leather boxes containing scripture) are kept secretly in his prison. He is allowed to read only *The New Testament* so that he can be converted to Christianity. Now he realises Russia "a complex, long suffering, ignorant, torn and helpless nation. In one sense, we all are prisoners here" (*The Fixer* 176). That is why he finds changes impossible to exist as he says, "The French have a saying, 'The more it changes, the more it remains the same'.... In effect it [society] has not changed in its essentials from what it was in the dim past, even though we tend loosely to think of civilisation as progress (*The Fixer* 173).

Nevertheless, Yakov's aforementioned realisation cannot be taken as his final observation. Though feeling frustrated from his life's tragedies in his terrified surroundings, he nearly gives in to the temptation of suicide, yet the realisation of a useless death and hope of a new life make him maintain his courage in the darkest time of his ordeal with no family to support him. He asserts, "... life is life and there's no sense kicking it into the grave" (*The Fixer* 77). "What do I get by dying, outside of release from pain? What have I earned if a single Jew dies because I did? Suffering I can gladly live without, I hate the taste of it, but if I must suffer, let it be for something. Let it be for Shmuel" (*The Fixer* 273). He gets relief from the thought that can continue living for Shmuel who he loves and respects. Moreover, Yakov decides, "If I live, sooner or later they'll have to bring me to trial. If not Nicholas the second, then Nicholas the Third will" (*The Fixer* 282). He rejects amnesty issued by the Tsars celebrating three-hundredth anniversary of the rule of his House of Ramanov for he does not wish to declare the Jews culprit before all Russia. His reading of the words "THE JEW IS DOOMED" (*The Fixer* 298) in the newspaper brings confidence in him when he finds many luminaries of literature, science and the professions, Kharkov Medical Society and press stand along with him in his favour (his lawyer Julius Ostrovsky also tells him). Yakov also succeeds in maintaining his sanity by reminding and talking to Raisl, Shmuel, his friends, Bibikov, the Tsar, etc. in his dreams and nightmares.

Malamud seems to be castigating the metanarrative of fidelity, chastity in marriage which does not work in a satisfactory way for both partners. This is seen in the episodes of Raisl's return almost three years after her elopement. Yakov's confidence doubles up when he finds Raisl back with him. Her keen desire to meet Yakov is visible when she appears before the Prosecuting Attorney five times for meeting Yakov who lets her meet him if she brings him around into signing the confession paper. Yakov, totally shattered in the mind and soul, accepts his deserter wife and her illegitimate son. On the one hand, Raisl's retreat to Yakov shows her helplessness to save herself and her child being called a "pariah" – the rejected one or outcaste (289) as the father of the child has deserted them. On the other, Raisl also emerges as the most daring and assertive woman when she wins the situation in her favour by making Yakov understand, "if you're going to judge me you'll have to judge me as I am" (*The Fixer* 285). In responding the complaining remark of Yakov "Once we were married you should have been faithful. A contract is a contract. A wife is a wife. Married is married" (*The Fixer* 285). Raisl equally raises the question before him, "Were you such a fine husband?" (*The Fixer* 286). She defends herself by saying:

> I slept with no one but you until you stopped sleeping with me. At twenty-eight I was too young for the grave. So, as you advised, I stopped being superstitious and at last took a chance. Otherwise I would soon have been dead. I was barren…. Whether I stayed or left I was useless to you, so I decided to leave. You wouldn't so I had to. I left in desperation to change my life.... It was either that or death, one sin or worse. I choose the lesser sin. (*The Fixer* 286)

He is able to prove that she is no longer barren and could have a baby. Her tears melt Yakov and he realises, "The last time I saw her she was crying like this, here she is still crying. In the meantime I've been two years in prison without cause, in solitary confinement, and chains. I've suffered freezing cold, filth, lice, the degradation of those searches, and she's still crying" (*The Fixer* 288).

Moreover, he accepts that she ran away because "she had tied herself to the wrong future [with Yakov]" (213). Yakov has already realised many of his mistakes in his dreams or nightmares which bring a change in him. Most frightening are those dreams in which his unfaithful Raisl suffer her repeated rapes amidst Jewish slaughter. When she runs in fear from Yakov, he finds himself a culprit who crushes the spirit of Raisl. He finds Raisl "a pretty girl, intelligent and dissatisfied, with even then a sad face" (*The Fixer* 209). He consoles her by saying:

> I've thought about our life from beginning to end and I can't blame you for more than I blame myself. If you give little you get less, though of some things I got more than I deserved.... I'm sorry I stopped sleeping with you. I was out to stab myself, so I stabbed you.... If I had my life to live over, you'd have less to cry about, so stop crying (*The Fixer* 286)

It also seems that having "softened towards Raisl, he gets a belated chance to nourish a 'new life' by acknowledging her illegitimate son as his own. The lad's name, appropriately, is *Chaim* or "life" (Siegel 136). Raisl's words, "Whoever acts the father is the father" (*The Fixer* 290), gives a call to the contemporary times where the kinship relations are no more important. The important is the mutual understanding and love and both accept it and he writes on the envelope of the confession paper, "I declare myself to be the father of Chaim, the infant son of my wife, Raisl Bok. He was conceived before she left me. Please help the mother and child, for this, amid all my troubles, I'll be grateful" (*The Fixer* 292).

Yakov at the signature place of the confession writes against authorities, "Every word is a lie" (292). The words of Raisl to Yakov "come home" shows the newly developed love relations between Raisl and Yakov, based on faith than on religion or marriage. Yakov becomes sad when he reminds, "Raisl has nothing to eat. I've never been of use to anybody and I'll never be" (*The Fixer* 326). Sometimes he "felt an overwhelming hunger to be back home [based on their mutual will and love], to see Raisl and set things straight, to decide what to do" (*The Fixer* 330), but he does not get orders.

Though the novel has an open ending as Yakov still waits for his freedom to go back to Raisl and his son, he feels his victory over the authorities. In order to produce terror in the minds of people, the authorities make the chained Yakov march through the streets of Kiev on the way to his trial. "It's the most they [Russian authorities] can do, and it's a lot" (Foer xi). However, Yakov finds himself freer than he was in the shtetl because he manages to resist confessing and finally receives an indictment and trial. So now he feels, "Something in myself has changed. I'm not the same man I was. I fear less and hate more" (*The Fixer* 319). His words, "there's no fight for it if there's no freedom" (*The Fixer* 335) and his slogan "Long live revolution! Long live liberty!" (*The Fixer* 335) point toward the present generation that cannot bear any exploitation and any domination because Yakov shows, "You can't sit still and see yourself destroyed" (*The Fixer* 335). He truly occupies a place among the postmodernists who consider it right to break off with the authority of family as well as with religious society unnecessarily enslaving human beings, because he says that he "wanted to live" (*The Fixer* 313).

The critical analysis of *The Fixer* shows that Malamud does go by neither authority nor its imposed rules. He sometimes congenially, sometimes ironically or sometimes bitterly raises his voice against metanarratives of parental authority, marriage convictions, the concept of God, the dictates of Judaism and Christianity binding human beings in chains. The core of Malamud's philosophy is the establishment of true relationships that can purely be based on love. In *The Fixer*, Yakov reconstructs his family ties with Raisl only because of his love for her.

Works Cited

Docherty, Thomas. "The Ethics of Alterity." *Postmodern Literary Theory: An Anthology*, edited by Niall Lucy. Blackwell, 2004, pp. 140-48.

Field, Leslie. "Saul Bellow: From Montreal to Jerusalem." *Studies in American Jewish Literature,* vol. 4, no. 2, 1978, pp. 51-59. *JSTOR*. www.jstor.org/stable/i4005405612. Accessed Nov. 2014.

Foer, Jonathan Saran. "Introduction." *The Fixer* by Bernard Malamud. Farrar, Straus and Giroux, 2004, pp. i-xi.

Handy, W. J. "The Malamud Hero: A Quest for Existence." *The Fiction of Bernard Malamud,* edited by Richard Astor and Jackson J. Benson. Affiliated East-West Press, 1992, pp. 65-86.

Hutcheon, Linda. *Historiographic Metafiction: Parody and the Intertextuality of History.* 1989, 12 Dec. 2013. *Tspace*, www.library.utoronto.ca/bitstream/1807/10252.

Malamud, Bernard. *The Fixer.* 1966. Farrar, Straus and Giroux, 2004.

Quart, Barbara Koenig. "Women in Bernard Malamud's Fiction." *Studies in American Jewish Literature*, vol. 3, 1983, pp. 138-50. *JSTOR*. www.jstor.org/stable/41205601. Accessed 18 Nov. 2011.

Siegel, Ben. "Through A Glass Darkly: Bernard Malamud's Painful View of the Self." *The Fiction of Bernard Malamud*, edited by Richard Astro and Jackson J. Benson. Affiliated East-West Press, 1992, pp. 117-48.

CHAPTER 4

Post-Modern Aesthetics in Contemporary American Literature: The Philosophy of Existentialism

Maroua Rogti

Giving answers to humans' questions and inquiries has always been the mission of philosophers and thinkers. They have always strived to provide explanations for everything. With each wave of thinkers and philosophers, new explanations appear whether to defeat previous thoughts, build on them, or prove them still valid to the currents of the time. At times, thinkers of the same period express contradicted views concerning the same issues. Existentialism and Postmodernism are one example. Although having coincided with same events, they were two different ways of thoughts in that they differ in their response to them; whereas Existentialism came to shed light on the individual as its central focus, Postmodernism treated the individual as anonymous, ambiguous, and living only in the present.

As wide as these two schools can be seen, a part of literature succeeded in merging between these two views putting the Postmodern individual in an Existential condition which is the subject matter of this study. This research is concerned with a theoretical groundwork on Existentialism and Postmodernism and the place of the postmodern individual. First, a general overview of Existentialism will be provided shedding light succinctly on central Existential concepts based on miscellaneous Existentialists' views. Then, a brief view about Postmodernism will be given, mainly, a historical background, followed by a highlight of the characteristics of the postmodern individual.

Like any way of thought, Existentialism grew up in a particular historical and cultural context. It came as a salvation to the confused and disoriented individual of its time whose insisting questions found no response in previous philosophies and ways of thought. Existentialism, as Solomon aptly puts it, "marks the ever-increasing failure of postmodern humanity to find itself "at home" in the world" (xii).

To quote Solomon, Existentialism was "the by-product of the Renaissance, the Reformation, the growth of science, the decline of Church authority, the French Revolution, the growth of mass militarism and technocracy, two world wars, the 'triumph' of capitalism, and the sudden onslaught of globalism and its consequences" (xii). As a result of all these events, people were in doubt and fear and lost confidence in everything. They found themselves in an objective rational and material world led by science and empiricism, and cares only about what is concrete, and no room was left for abstract things such as fear, love, and ethics.

People faced this world with no trustworthy religion to refer to with the decline of the church, not even science was convincing for them to explain the brutalities of the two world wars, and they were no more treated as individuals but as small entities of a much bigger globe. This triggered in them many daring abstract questions such as: what is the meaning of our lives? Why does the individual meet death? What ethics is the world led by? What is the source of those ethics? Do we even need ethics? Are we the product of our society or should we meet our impulses? Shall we act as entities in that unfair world or act as individuals? (Cogswell).That was what Existentialism came to address to. It came to help people to understand the world better, and find meaning to their lives as individuals. That is the uniqueness of Existentialism in contrast to previous philosophies; being by the side of the individual, being what Sartre describes it "a doctrine which makes human life possible" (32).

According to Collins' dictionary, Existentialism is defined as "a modern philosophical movement stressing the importance of personal experience and responsibility and the demands that they make on the individual, who is seen as a free agent in a deterministic and seemingly meaningless universe" ("Existentialism"). From this definition, one can understand that Existentialism sheds light on the individual who has the freedom to control his own experiences and choices despite living in an absurd world. More simply, one can say that Existentialism is the philosophy of the individual.

Panza & Gale also provide a detailed explanation to the term 'Existentialism' explaining how it is particularly concerned with human existence:

> A more technical definition of existentialism reveals the reason for its name. Existentialism is the study of existence. If you take existence to be everything that exist – such as chairs and tables, people and llamas – all philosophy, science, and religion would seem to have the same subject. But existentialism isn't the study of everything that exists; it's the study of existence itself – the study of what it means for something to exist at all as opposed to not existing. It's also the study of what it means for something, as opposed to nothing, to exist at all. Ofcourse, the primary focus of existentialism is a particular kind of existence, the kind of existence that includes existing things like you, because you're aware of your existence and capable of questioning it. (13)

This definition clarifies that Existentialism is concerned not with the verb 'to exist' which involves all subjects but with the noun 'existence' as a vivid quality. This quality is more valuable of study in humans as being the only existing creatures who are conscious about their existence and can put it into thought.

In what follows, main Existential concepts will be discussed from different Existentialists' views, namely, Soren Kierkegaard (1813-1855), Jean Paul Sartre (1905-1980), Martin Heidegger (1889-1976), and Albert Camus (1913-1960). These concepts were chosen as the central ones into explaining the philosophy of Existentialism for two reasons. On one hand, these concepts provide the basis into which Existentialists build their views to understand human existence. On the other hand, because they are interrelated and overlapping, they, together, form one core idea about Existentialism through which other Existential concepts can easily be understood such as freedom, responsibility, despair, alienation, bad faith, and death.

It is the core conception upon which Existentialism (contemporary atheistic Existentialism) is built upon, and the principle that differentiates it from pervious philosophies. This idea of self-creation originates from the view that God is dead. Since there is no God, no creature who determines the essence of human beings before their existence, as atheistic Existentialists like Sartre and Heidegger believe, there is no unified human nature everyone should adopt. Therefore, it is the individual's responsibility to create his own essence subjectively (Grene).

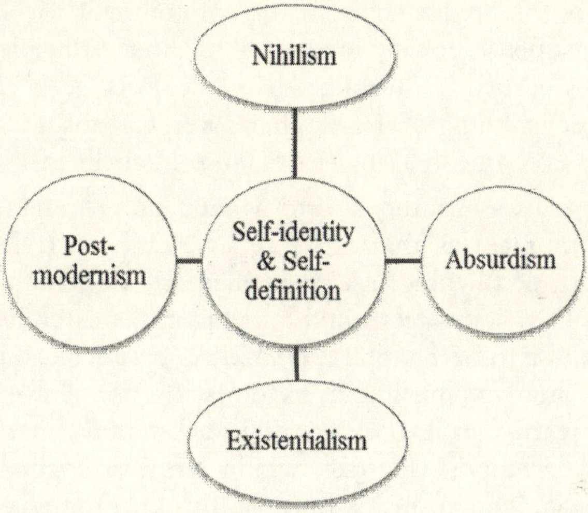

Figure 1. Existentialist Philosophy

Sartre asserts that, "by 'existence precedes essence' we mean that man first exists: he materialises in the world, encounters himself, and only afterward defines himself" (22). Sartre believes that human beings, unlike other beings, come to the world with the total freedom to make themselves. In other words, they exist first in the world, then they find their essence; it is not predefined or determined by any other force. This quality stems from human beings' perception as self-conscious and free creatures who have the capacity of determining the type of persons they will be. However, Sartre does not illuminate the effect of the environment one exists in, which he calls 'facticity'. He believes that humans practice their freedom within the limitations of their 'facticity'. Their capacity of creating their essence lays on their freedom of interpreting the surrounding world according to who they are and who they want to be (Wicks).

For Kierkegaard and Sartre, the absurd is defined in terms of human beings' actions and choices as they result from humans' freedom. The fact that these choices and actions are unique to individual experiences and views is what makes their absurdity. They are absurd for if taken outside the individual situation, they cannot be reasonably justified. Kierkegaard explains this by reference to the biblical story of Abraham and Isaac. He believes that Abraham's decision of sacrificing his son

Isaac, accompanied with the belief that he will have him back by the grace of God, is originated from his commitment to God's faith and cannot be justified rationally by outside religious principles because it is related to his particular situation. His choice was freely taken based on his own understanding of faith. Therefore, it is absurd and cannot be generated to everyone in a similar situation (Michelman).

For Albert Camus the absurd is not only human's actions and choices, it embraces all that exists i.e. everything is running without a purpose or plan; all things are unjustified. He is perhaps the best one who tackles this view directly and in detail in his extended essay on the absurd, "The Myth of Sisyphus" (1942). As he puts it, the absurd is the result of the human's intrinsic need to make sense of everything around once faced by the meaningless world. To quote him, "man stands face to face with the irrational. He feels within him his longing for happiness and for reason. The absurd is born of this confrontation between the human need and the unreasonable silence of the world" (20).

Through the story of Sisyphus, Camus guides us to the best way of dealing with the absurd. He considers Sisyphus as the ideal absurd hero who becomes happy once he accepts that his life is nothing but that absurd struggle of rolling the rock up the mountain and having it roll back down once he reaches the top. He believes that the best way to face the absurd is embracing it i.e. accepting the fact that we are living a meaningless and purposeless life. He assumes that this is the only way humans can find happiness.

Anxiety is an important concept for Existentialists, for they consider it a significant mood into human understanding of his existence. It takes different labels such as dread, anguish, and angst, based on different translations (Michelman). Before digging deeper into how different Existentialists explain it, it is necessary to differentiate it from fear, a concept or a mood that is usually confused with it.

First, fear is different from anxiety in that it is usually related to a specific object, for example, height, cats, dogs, etc.; whereas, anxiety is about no specific object, it is about existence itself. Second, as a result of the first point, fear can be discovered easily once faced by the object provoking it; whereas, anxiety, for being related to nothing, not to a worldly object, it cannot be easily recognised. In short, fear is an 'everyday mood' whereas anxiety is an 'Existential mood' (Panza and Gale). The latter property explains why Existentialists consider anxiety an essential mood into existence understanding.

Kierkegaard describes anxiety as "the dizziness of freedom," that feeling of uneasiness humans encounter when they are on the verge of choices and possibilities. The human feels anxious not because of choices but because of the freedom they have over these choices, and the responsibility that results from this freedom (Gordon). As usual, he explains this concept from a religious perspective as related to the experience of sin; yet considers it a necessary step in the formation of the authentic spiritual identity (Michelman). This latter, he thinks, undergoes three stages: the aesthetic, then the ethical, and finally the religious. Anxiety, for him, is a necessary step to move to the final stage which to reach it, people make a "leap of faith." This leap of faith is where the individual embraces his freedom to choose between good and bad. Therefore, he encounters a "dizziness of freedom," he becomes anxious (Panza and Gale 68).

Like Kierkegaard, Heidegger considers anxiety as an important step towards authenticity. In everyday life, the human acts in the world harmoniously with its rules, principles, and systems. However, this life, although being comfortable and frees the human from the responsibility of making choices of his own, is not authentic and does not reflect the human's real self. Here comes the role of anxiety. It helps the human recognise that the world, he is acting in comfortably, is meaningless i.e. absurd. As a result, he starts thinking of his being as an independent free entity responsible for its choices and for giving an authentic meaning to his life (Critchley).

Another aspect related to anxiety, according to Heidegger, is death. At the moment the human recognises death as his potential possibility, not an outside experience only sensed by others, he becomes anxious. This anxiety is not negative; it rather helps the human live more authentically. As he embraces death as an inevitable possibility, he starts to act freely in the face of every day's possibilities (Magrini). Thus, in Heidegger's view, anxiety is the human's sense of his being-in-the-world, his freedom, and his being-towards-death.

Sartre agrees with Kierkegaard and Heidegger that anxiety is the human sense of freedom. This is noted in his famous saying "man is condemned to be free" (Sartre 29). Human experiences anxiety as he acknowledges his freedom and the responsibility resulting from it. Sartre describes the sense of freedom as condemnation as most people tend to deny it to avoid the feeling of anxiety and the pressure of responsibilities resulting from embracing freedom. This denial of human individuality and his power to bring change to the world by the virtue of freedom is what Sartre calls "bad faith." It is the human confession that his character is determined by the world he acts in, not by his own choices, which is only a defensive mechanism against anxiety (Webber).

Sartre considers anxiety not only the result of human responsibility and freedom of choice, but of another extended responsibility he assigns to human beings. He believes that when taking any action, one ought to think that his action is reflected in humanity as a whole. He explains this through the example of a military leader whose decisions influence not only him but all the soldiers following him. This choice is no doubt a source of anxiety as it reflects humanism and the power of the individual to create values for the world.

Authenticity, for Kierkegaard, means living a religious life, which is the final and ultimate stage in life one can only reach by embracing the absurdity of existence through a leap of faith (Gordon). Kierkegaard believes that most people live dispute in the first two stages of life, the aesthetic and the ethical. In the first stage i.e. the aesthetic, people are totally passive in taking control over their lives, do not question their existence, deny their freedom of choice, and live only for momentous pleasure; a life that does not reflect who they are.

As people start questioning their existence and making choices about their life, they jump into the second stage, the ethical. In this stage, people tend to join a social or ethical system of rules and take a side that determines who they are in life. However, they are still inauthentic, in Kierkegaard's view, as life is absurd and cannot be explained through a set of rules of one certain system. For him, meaning is only found in one's relationship with God, not in the world; as people capture this, they reach the final authentic religious stage of life. At the point they take responsibility for their lives and face the absurdity of existence with God's faith, not with worldly ethical rules; they become authentic (Panza & Gale).

The same as Kierkegaard, Heidegger thinks that everyday life most people are absorbed into is not authentic. As people live within society and abide by its rules and principles, although feel comfortable and relieved, they are deprived of assuming their freedom to choose how to live true to who they are and take responsibility for their choices (Golomb). Therefore, authenticity stands at the opposite state, the state in which people sense their existence as independent and free entities responsible for their own lives. This can be attained, according to Heidegger, only by embracing death as one's personal experience and ultimate possibility which requires encountering anxiety. Hence, authenticity, in Heidegger's mind, is found in human's understanding of his relation to death and his being in the world as a being-into-death (Michelman).

Sartre contradicts with Heidegger about considering death as the source of meaning of life but agrees with him that assuming one's freedom is a necessary step toward authenticity (Gordon). Sartre actually has less to say about authenticity, but is the best one to be cited when talking about inauthenticity for he describes it through real examples:

> The café waiter who tries to assume the "being" of his social role, to actually "be" a waiter and not merely "play at" being one; the homosexual who accepts society's judgment that he is determined to act according to a specific human "type"; the idealistic woman who evades her sexuality by dissociating her true self (her mind) from her body (her hand) being caressed by a suitor. (Michelman 44)

In each of the previous cases, the individual is pursuing a "bad faith" which is the state of escaping oneself and avoiding accepting the reality of one's freedom of choice and the responsibility of it. In the three cases above, each is living according to outside judgment and roles not according to their real selves. Each one is escaping his reality and embracing an outside one, just to avoid the responsibility resulting from being true to who they are. That is what Sartre calls "bad faith" and that is what means to live disputants (Flynn).

For Camus, the only way to live authentically is to accept and embrace the absurdity of life. Yet, this acceptance is not an act of surrender, but of revolt. It is a courageous act of creating one's own meaning to life and defending it in the face of a meaningless world. Camus explains his understanding of authenticity, although rarely using the term, through the myth of Sisyphus. He believes that since the moment Sisyphus accepts the meaninglessness of his repeated action of rolling the rock to the top of the mountain, then having it rolling down to start all over again, he revolts against the fact that it is a punishment. He creates his own meaning of this act by courageously embracing it; as a result, he starts to live authentically. Camus thinks that the attitude of Sisyphus is the only authentic attitude one can proudly take in revolt against the absurd life; as a result, attains happiness (Golomb).

Ultimately, Existentialists' views together, inauthenticity is human's passive immersion into everyday activities that are determined by the rules and systems of the society he/she lives in, without seeking meaning for his/her existence or making personal choices. On the other hand, authenticity is the state of being ones' original self that runs a life based on individual choices; a state in which one embraces the absurdity of life and acknowledges his/her freedom and responsibility to give meaning to life.

In the late twentieth century turn and after the end of the World War II, the world has witnessed prominent changes in society, especially in both technology and science: nuclear weapons, mass media, telecommunication, and information technology (internet in particular) that turned it into a small village where knowledge is available to almost everyone under the umbrella of industrialisation. These reactionary and evolutionary changes led to question the role of culture and art as well.

Accordingly, recent and new social, political, and literary theories have appeared to include a variety of disciplines such as art, architecture, film, sociology, communication, and philosophy. Therefore, one of the intriguingly significant literary movements that have currently come to existence is Postmodernism. The latter represents a completely new paradigm in intellectual terminology and thought. From a philosophical perspective, it anchors the breakdown of certainty i.e. there is no absolute truth as "human is the product of history and society and rationality rather than being a natural endowment is a historical cultural outcome and the stream of thought" (Farhangpour and Abdolsalami). Indeed, one of the postmodern themes is the rejection of "universal objective truth" which is apparently stated by Jean-Francois Lyotard "incredulity towards metanarratives". According to postmodernists, there is no universal "Truth" instead there are only "truths" that are special to a certain society or group of people and restricted to individual perception (Veerachary).

According to Elaati, Postmodernism envelops new ideas about history in a particular time and place. It basically seeks to reduce the significance of history paying less attention to its value and role as regarded as a witness to what is going on and recording facts. However, stories may be wrong and the witness always testifies the strong side. It considers the pursuit of the ultimate truth as rather a mistaken claim and Postmodernism basically calls for the impossibility to reach the truth.

The Postmodern narrative often focuses on both the author as well as the reader, however, Postmodernists try to take the voice from the author to give the floor to the readers to interpret texts; as stated by Rosenau "No longer is the reader a passive subject to be entertained, instructed, or amused. S/he is given the freedom to attribute meaning to the text without consequence or responsibility" (25). This never means that the reader's voice is the privileged one since each reader interprets the same literary dialogue differently. Even though the author's voice has been taken away, he is still free to produce text, even if they are individually interpreted by different readers.

Lyotard appoints that scientific knowledge never represents the totality of knowledge. The same can be applied to the social and cultural perspective simply because one being or culture does not represent the wholeness of communities. According to Rosenau, the postmodern individual "will have an almost anonymous existence. S/he will be a person but will not be held accountable for events, actions, and outcomes; nor will s/he be the author of "caring" relationships (humanist) or creative individualism. S/he will be so independent of all identifiable truth seeking perspectives that s/he is, in short, no subject at all" (53). That is to say, the postmodern being generally has an ambiguous life where s/he is not responsible for events, actions, and outcomes.

Rosenau mentions some features of the Postmodern individual as being "relaxed and flexible" directed towards "feelings and emotions, exteriorisation" and believing in "a be-yourself attitude". The postmodern being is a vivid human being making his own version of social reality "pursuing a personal quest for meaning" and "preferring the temporary over the permanent, s/he is contented with a "live and let live" (in the present) attitude" (54). It means that the postmodern being calls for immediate pleasure. He favours spontaneity over planning. According to Rosenau, the postmodern beings are more interested in their own lives, their personal satisfaction and self-promotion, less interested in social institutions like marriage, family, church and nation and directed more to their personal needs.

In our times, the modern individual seems less interested in the integration of his/her diverse social roles and experiences into a unity, but rather, the modern individual calls for internalising the external, pluralism of norms, beliefs, and values. The modern beings also attempt to achieve a meaningful life simply because they are uncertain about what is meaningful in life and what is not? (Reichenbach)

Postmodern individuals have adopted new values, beliefs, behaviours, and attitudes compared to their modern counterpart (Inkeles, et. al.). Inglehart identifies postmodern individuals as those who are highly subjective and who believe in secular-rational authority over traditional one. They make such a shift from traditional authority because they prefer independence and freedom. Besides, behaviours and attitudes might be affected by material conditions; as long as they indicate a broader social environment. Bauman declares:

> Postmodernity does not seek to substitute one truth for another, one standard of beauty for another, one life ideal for another. Instead, it splits the truth, the standards and the ideal into already deconstructed and about to be deconstructed. It denies in advance the right of all and any revelation to slip into the place vacated by the deconstructed/discredited rules. It braces itself for a life without truths, standards and ideals. (09)

It is actually the same the way the postmodern being lives, as he does not prefer one absolute truth, but rather he believes that the truth may not always be recognised and actual ideals should be questioned. Although postmodernity braces itself for a life without truths, standards and ideals, the postmodern being follows the same path. In the absence of truths, he is not able to set ideals that definitely lead to never consider truths in the future; consequently, he, basically, lives in the present.

In a postmodern world full of contradictions and discrepancies, the individual dives in a sea of uncertainties where his mind starts to question almost all the mainstream conventions including all life's aspects. He even suspects the essence of his existence. Therefore, Postmodernism and Existentialism, as schools of thought, come to provide a cogent explanation to the modern beings' attitudes and thoughts. The postmodern individual grows in a world where truth is not one, where he has no voice, and the only time he can question is his present. At that time, Existentialists came to shed light on him. They treat him as a free individual responsible for his life. They consider him as the only one responsible for creating meaning. They give him more dimensions as an individual tied to the past, present, and future, not only a present creature. At last, they provide him with the solutions to face and cope with that absurd world that rejects absolute truths. In short, Existentialism came to highlight the individual that Postmodernism treats as anonymous. On the other hand, postmodernism, as it believes in no absolute truth, made the Postmodern being skeptic about everything around. It doubts systems, rules, and standards, and prefers to create its own meaning of life subjectively. As a result, the postmodern individual is characterised by being spontaneous and seeking immediate pleasure. He is the one that favours his own interests and his own self-promotion and satisfaction irrespective of the outcomes and of the rules and systems of the society.

Works Cited

Bauman, Zygmunt. *Intimations of Postmodernity*. Routledge, 1992.

Camus, Albert. *The Myth of Sisyphus and Other Essays*. Translated by Justin O'Brien, Vintage, 1955.

Cogswell, David. *Existentialism for Beginners*. Steerforth Press, 2008.

Critchley, Simon. "Being and Time, Part 05: Anxiety." *The Guardian*, www.theguardian.com/commentisfree/belief/2009/jul/06/heidegger-philosophy-being. Accessed 07 January 2021.

Elaati, Abdulazim N. "Postmodern Theory." 2016, doi:10.13140/RG.2.1.4515.0327.

Farhangpour, Yasaman and Atefeh Abdolsalami. "The Philosophy of Postmodernism, Its Scholars and Its Impact on Art." *International Conference on Research in Art*, 2016, pp. 01-15.

Flynn, Thomas. *Existentialism: A Very Short Introduction*. OUP, 2006.

Golomb, Jacob. *In Search of Authenticity: Existentialism From Kierkegaard to Camus*. Routledge, 1995.

Gordon, Haim, editor. *Dictionary of Existentialism*. Greenwood Press, 1999.

Grene, Marjorie. *Dreadful Freedom*. U of Chicago P, 1948.

Inkeles, Alex, et. al. "Becoming Modern: Individual Change in Six Developing Countries." *Contemporary Sociology*, vol. 05, no. 02, 1976, pp.118-20, doi: 10.2307/2062924

Michelman, Stephen. *Historical Dictionary of Existentialism*. Scarecrow Press, Inc., 2008.

Panza, Christopher and Gregory Gale. *Existentialism for Dummies*. Wiley Publishing, Inc., 2008.

Reichenbach, Roland. "The Postmodern Self and the Problem of Developing a Democratic Mind." *Theory & Research in Social Education*, vol. 26, no. 02, 1998, pp. 226-37, doi.org/10.1080/00933104.1998.10505845.

Rosenau, Pauline. *Postmodernism and the Social Sciences*. Princeton UP, 1991.

Sartre, Jean-Paul, et. al. *Existentialism is a Humanism*, edited by John Kulka, Annotated, Yale UP, 2007.

Solomon, Robert. *Existentialism*. OUP, 2005.

Veerachary, P. "Philosophical Dimensions of Postmodernism." *International Journal of Humanities and Social Science Invention*, vol. 07, no. 05, 2018, pp. 32-37.

Webber, Jonathan. *The Existentialism of Jean-Paul Sartre*. Routledge, 2009.

Wicks, Robert. *Modern French Philosophy: From Existentialism to Postmodernism*. One World, 2003.

CHAPTER 5

Dichotomous Worlds in Joanna Russ' *The Female Man*

Urmil Rawat

The present paper explores the cultural conflict of gender roles in the text *The Female Man* of Joanna Russ (1937-2011), a feminist science fiction writer. The study focuses on utopian and dystopian state to realise the possibility to confront the patriarchal mindset. Utopian and dystopian notion creates an ideal ground for challenging the prevalent gender roles in the society constructed by the cultural approval of it. The challenge is in the form of rejection, greater degree of acceptance or oblivion of such roles. The gender will be studied in isolation and in relation to the other, with the thought process going into the praxis of their creation and sustenance by judging their vitality. The emphasis in both the worlds is on future feminist evolution. Feminist utopia is a place where women are not judged, governed or discriminated on the basis of their gender. It is a world with equal distribution of opportunities, rights and duties. It negates the dictate of the existing culture that women are to assist and sustain men to the point of subservience. Hence it is a visualised state which proves to be a catalyst in cultural conflict. Dystopia on the contrary, is a world in which gender inequalities breed and women are too frail to grapple with the cultural shell to condone it. Feminist science fiction is the platform to portray women in its widest range with varied themes, hitherto unexplored.

In these modern complicated times, women are evolving. They are constantly experimenting with new set of identities evolving around feminist notion of substance, empowerment, and emancipation. There is dissatisfaction among women due to gender roles constructed universally over the ages. Acculturation is inherent in every step of child's growth to adulthood. In the case of female child her psyche can be understood only through her sexuality which shapes her, so the aim is to unravel the intertwining threats of unenigmatic female sexuality as well as socio-cultural aspect of it. She is influenced by righteous conduct as dictated by religion and society. The delicate balance between female expectations and those that are actually fulfilled, is addressed in the study. Multitasking a cultivated trait in women has enabled great strides but at times also holds a disadvantageous position. Our culture has proactive rule in figuring women's role but has been unable to keep pace with changing socio-economic scenario. The conflict ensuing has not developed overnight but has been gradually gaining momentum over a period of time. Although unfairness of gender has been fought by feminist from the outset, its recognition has been greater with the advent of technology and social media in the private domain. Gender and culture are closely connected to each other. Culture mentor sensitises gender characteristic and behaviour. It enables construction of identities and relationships. Brian Attebery has insight of relationship between gender and culture:

> It is rooted in biology but shaped by culture to such a degree that it is impossible to untwist the thread and say which strands are unborn and which are acquired and arbitrary. There is no natural gender any more than there is a natural language (3).

The feminist has always complained that language is gendered and visible in all cultures. Men and women are taught to speak differently. The arduous journey toward gender equality was undertaken by American women before the legitimacy of their voice, their rights and their acceptance of being separate identity of their own. Feminists believe that women sexuality has been moulded by patriarchy for its own survival. Female physiology is quite different from male one. It is ironical although contemporary times are seen as liberal and progressive, and yet when compared to the ancient times, it appears restraint and regressive. Feminist utopia is the transitional milestone to achieve women centric customs, symbol, belief, language, culture of their own. Feminist utopia is the creation of women who do not need men for their validation. It is egalitarian world having dynamics achievable through logic and reasoning with semblance of perfection.

The novel follows the lives of four women living in parallel fictional worlds that differ in time and place. When they enter into each other's world, their pre-existing notions of womanhood is shaken. Russ explores different views on gender roles making them assess their lives and their womanhood. She highlights women by contrasting in four parallel worlds. She presents "four version of same woman" Joanna, Jeannine, Janet and Jael. The idea is to explore and demonstrate the opportunities, life and identity of a woman in the society. As Jael introduces, they shared same autonomic nervous system, adrenals, hair, teeth, eyes, circulatory system with same innocence," we ought to think alike, and feel alike, act alike but of course we don't "(Russ 156). Jeannine is the youngest hailing from earth where great depression has not ended; Joanna is somewhat older and is from earth of the 1970's; Janet is a native of Whileaway, the feminist utopia hardier than the two due to "her life out doors a Swedish hiker and a farm hand"(Russ 155), and so is disease worry free. Jael is from a dystopia where men and women are constantly engaged in a conflict.

The text begins with description of Janet's utopian world, Whileaway which is matriarchal world as a strange plague had engulfed Whileaway which was gender specific in nature and targeted male species thus wiping them out. Love, sex, marriage and family are experienced within the same sex. Janet is married and has two children. Joanna is in an attempt to help Janet get aware and accustom to other sex, takes her to a party where she would meet men "the first uncontrolled contact with the beastly savages" (Russ 34). Women in the party are epitome of the subscribed gender roles, the different archetypes of femininity. Russ through party showcases the patriarchal, sexual attitude prevalent in the society. The male voices vary in statement but not in essence. A passing male remarked "you women are lucky, you don't have to go out and go to work" (Russ 35).

The society in Whileaway has no patriarchal influence, there are no set rules or attitudes dictated in the field of romance. Sexuality is explored within the same sex. No power and prominence has room within such a relationship. Acceptance and acknowledgement of sexuality and sex enables the Whileawanyans to possess technologically sex toy. This acceptability is sufficient to break the stereotypical walls for heterosexuality forever. Joanna tells Jeannie it would ruin her mind and make her crazy: "You will be lost to respectability and decency, decorum and dependency and all sorts of nice normal things beginning with D. It will kill you, Jeannie. You will be dead, dead, dead" (Russ 144).

The variance in personalities and attitudes in four "Js" is too conspicuous to ignore and overlook. This discrepancy can be attributed to socio-cultural factors in the society. Janet has two mothers as parents. She has been taught the ways of combatant both psychically and psychologically. She had multiple vocations before reaching the age of

30. She had worked in the mines, on the radio network, a milk farm, a vegetable farm, as a librarian, delivered babies, fixed machineries, supervised digging of fire trails and even fought combats, "I have fought four duels. I have killed four times". (Russ 2) Janet was the first traveler to make the contact with Jeannine and Joanna. When Janet is enquired about the killing of men, she replied that habit dictate such urges. When probed about the return to Whileaway, she innocently asks "why?" As she doesn't feel the requirement of the opposite gender in her world. When told "one sex is half a species, Miss Evason" (Russ 10). Do you think we are missing out on something use by not having men? She retorts, "I am married, I have two children, what the devil do you mean?" (Russ 10).

Russ paints Whileaway in eco-feminist colour. As an agricultural society, lot of technology is invested to increase production. Transportation is eco-friendly. Monorail is for long distance traveling while bicycle has a ubiquitous presence. Industry was drastically altered with invention of the" induction helmet" which makes it possible for one workwoman to have not only the brute force but also the flexibility and control of thousands" (Russ 13).

Russ provides Jeannine, Joanna and Jael as foil to Janet. As a 29-year-old librarian, Jeannine is torn between society's expectations and her own subconscious desire to live on her own terms. She is a caricature of Janet. She is under tremendous pressure to cherish womanhood by being a wife and a mother. Her character is pitiable as she tries to love up to the expectations set by herself, her brother, her mother. She thinks constantly her desire to be married and have a husband. She is stuck in a relationship with Cal who is not assertive. Jeannine always tries to evade and escape him. The love making is a mechanical act for her to which she only agrees after he frowns and pleads continuously. Jeannine is a highly intelligent woman and sick of having her existence marked out by men. She spontaneously decides to marry Cal for the sake of family but later reneges on her engagement after meeting Jael, a kindred spirit. She goes a step ahead by joining clarion call of Jael to liberate women from their gender roles by a revolution in the end.

It is difficult to describe the character of Joanna, as she jumps from one role to other seamlessly. Sometimes she is a narrator and sometimes an all-pervading spirit. Joanna felt to forget her identity of a woman and becomes a man, to ensure that her rightful place is given to her. She doesn't believe in inferiority of women, but realises the acceptance and equality of a woman is an anomaly, which every quarter is tried to be rectified and put to her rightful subjugated place so she understands that salvation lies in her adopting the male role, "I had just changed into a man, me, Joanna. I mean a female man, of-course my body and soul were exactly the same." (Russ 5) If a woman is denied a right to be equal because of her gender, she should simply change into acceptable one, not in essence but have a veneer of it as Russ describes:

> For years I have been saying Let me in, Love me, Approve me, Define me, Regulate me, Validate me, Support me. Now, I say Move over. If we all are Mankind it follows to my interested and righteous and right now very beady little eyes that I too am a Man not a Woman.... I think I am a man; I think you had better call me a man; I think you will write about me as a Man from now on and speak of me as a man and employ me as a man and recognise child rearing as a man's business; you will think of me as a Man and treat me as a Man... If you don't by all the god and saints, I'll break your neck. (135-36)

The youngest in the group with" Js" is Laura Rose Wilding, a seventeen-year-old, "pathologically shy" (Russ 58) girl. Without being aware of being Whileaway she could easily be part of feminist utopia. She refuses a gender role of a female. She believes that she is a victim of "penis envy" so can never be happy and can lead a normal life (Russ 64). The eminent Austrian psychologist Sigmund Freud believed that the shaping of the human personality was the outcome of the events that unfolded in the childhood. It is the unconscious which is the most powerful drive influencing behaviour and cognition. Freud's Oedipus complex, Electra complex, dream analysis, views on "castration" and "penis envy" made it impossible for any person, no matter the age, gender and association (relation) to escape it. The entire gamut of instinct, libido and personality are laid on biological aspect by Freud. Karen Horney, his apprentice, refuted his obsession with sexual nature of a being and contested by her, "There is no evidence, for instance, that the tenderness between mother and child is a sexual nature" (Horney 148). According to her article, "Culture and Neurosis" the society places impediments in the natural growth of a child, making child feel conflicted, anxious and unable to adapt. So a neurotic is born due to "difficulties caused by the conflicting character of demands which a culture imposes on its individuals" (416).

Laura merely wants recognition as a person which is denied to her. Her quest for recognition ends when she met Janet. Laura is attracted towards Janet being fully aware that sexual relationship with same sex is not conventional in her world. Love reciprocates love. Taboo is not broken by Laura alone, Janet too being guilty of it. In Whileaway homosexuality was the norm but cross generational relationship was not. The huge age difference between them made the relationship off – limits even in Whileaway. The violation however brings positive transformation especially for Laura. Jael is native of dystopian earth and here world is in midst of an ongoing war for past 40 years between men and women "Us and Them" (Russ 157).

Jael unlike other "Js" is not emotional or weak in knees, she is go – getter and believes in women being more equal than men. Jael decided that women should rule not only in her world but in other worlds as well. She has brought all the"' Js" in her world to force recognition on them, to make them aware that apart them is not happy with their identities, being stomped upon, "truth is that people don't recognise themselves accept in mirror and sometime not even then". (Russ 156). She wants "Js" to have their own clandestine bases in their world and work for an uprising to throw away patriarchy vehemently and start a new era of women's rule. In the end, living Janet, Jael is able to brainwash other Js to be her foot soldiers in impending war against male species. Her tirade against the men even changes the demeanour of her followers. Jeannie and Joanna exhibit implicit faith in Jael's declaration of a violent revolution for women emancipation: "Goodbye to everything. Goodbye to Janet, whom we don't believe in and whom we derided but who is in secret our savior from utter despair…." (Russ 206).

This valediction is the start of a new beginning in a phase of revolt resultant of culturally segregated gender roles. Saviour is Janet because she has shown them the reality of a woman based utopia where one can live without the undermining of one's identity and potential. It is evident that gender roles agitate and upset Jael and Joanna but there is difference in their reaction. Joanna superficially decides to become male gender and play the role to her benefit whereas Jael reverses gender role, she becomes a man. At home Jael keeps Davy, an ideal homemaker who makes and serves drink to guests. He is reduced to a sensual object by the detail of his physical attribute especially of being the most "beautiful man" (Russ 178). He is a controlled puppet of Jael, having minimal action of eating, sleeping or eliminating on his own. Janet is a product of feminist utopian world, but that doesn't make her exceptional in any way. She has her own quirks and set of eccentricities that make her common relatable. Although biology places her with Joanna and Jeannie but her thinking, attitude and deportment makes her a foil to them. In

Whileaway there is no duality of gender, making it impossible for Janet to fathom the role performed by women and men.

The constant shift in narratives enables Russ to demonstrate that it is not the narrative of one woman alone. In fact, that all the women feel stifled under the engagement rules of patriarchy. In every walk of life, they are made to remember physical feebleness which gets translated in competency, a flaw in working and character. As the story progresses it is Jael holding the centre stage with her revolutionary vision and towards the end of the novel, the views of other three gains momentum. It is interesting that by depicting Jeannie's past as dystopian and Joanna's world as similar to her world, Russ shows her disappointment and disapproval of the past. The remedy which she presents is in form of Janet's world Whileaway achievable only through attempts of activist like Jael. It is worth noting that the resident of the utopia, Janet is not convinced of Jael and doesn't approve of her methods. The relationship which both share is complementary, to dislike of Janet. Finally Jael, the saviour of Jeannine, infuses fresh life in her decaying identity. Jeannine transforms into a confident woman, aware of her choices. In the similar fashion Laura too changes to an assertive woman who is confident of her sexuality. Both join Jael in her revolutionary version of social change.

The study of feminist utopia and dystopia provides us with all the solution to reconstitute the society devoid of gender roles inflicting the contemporary times. It provides vistas for the reader to distinguish the worth and necessity of either gender. It lays stress in the cordiality between sexes otherwise scarier version of society is in store. It appears that utopia and dystopia are each other's nemesis, for one to succeed other must be defeated yet both are related to each other. Only in absence of one, other is present. They are imperative to each other. In isolation the contraries do not exist, similar to the concept of Yin and Yang. The failure of utopia leads to dystopia whereas dystopia always paves way for utopian aspirations. The prevailing gender roles are maladaptive to the times. For our survival and growth we need our souls to be saturated with hope of an imminent futuristic utopia that will see us with our best foot forward willing to let go our obstinacy and flaws. Culture needs a face lift, a revival bringing it in tune with evolutionary pace of life. Society has to work cohesively as a unit to compact the forces of segregation raising the embitterment which is not conducive for harmonious living.

Works Cited

Attebery, Brian. *Decoding Gender in Science Fiction.* Routledge, 2002.

Horney, Karen. "Culture and Nemesis." *American Sociological Review,* vol.1, no.2, 1936, pp. 221-30.

Russ, Joanna. *The Female Man.* Orion Publishing Group, 2010.

CHAPTER 6

American Railways in the Time of Postmodernism: A Discourse on Contemporary Literature

Sudipta Sardar

The history of American railways is almost two centuries old. The first railway in America was introduced in 1827 for commercial transport of passengers and freight. The introduction of the railways brought much excitement and elation because of its multifarious importance and usefulness. Thus the literature of the mid-nineteenth century presented railways as the pathfinder of a new generation and a messenger of a new peace civilisation. Most of the literature of the times, for example Walt Whitman's poetry, presented railways as the light bringer in the darkness, amidst dense and dark forest of American untrodden lands. But the destruction and faithlessness in the passenger railway vehicles came after the introduction of a strong political and economical outlook which wanted the railways to provide more profit. American railways had been one of those railways having an age old history and a tremendous amount of impact on the civilisation and society. It needed to be mentioned that the history of American railways had been a fascinating story. The development of railroads by the earliest European civilisation was going in a full flow in the beginning of the nineteenth century. The railroads proved to be too crucial for the new nation of America. Apparently, it could be said that the impact that the railways had on the lives of American people at that time, was unimaginable. It proved to be their sole carrier to prosperity and development.

In the nineteenth century American literature, the same impetuous and glory of railways could be found very easily. Walt Whitman, Henry David Thoreau and Emerson, all sang the glory of the American railways. The railways were like water in the desert for the lives of the American people in the nineteenth century. The rapidity and tremendous amount of growth of the railways impacted the social and industrial growth of the American people. The railways had been their sole carrier of prosperity and development in the nineteenth century but the end of the nineteenth century and the World Wars devastated the growth and development of the railways. In the first half of the twentieth century, American railways started to decay and took the backstage, whereas much impetus was given to the roads by the then political leaders. In the aftermath of the world wars, the dream fullfilling railways became a rusty and unused phenomenon. Thus in the postmodern era, particularly after the 1960s the railways ceased to be of the first and foremost importance. Though, several crucial steps were taken to reawaken the long dead dreamy atmosphere of the railways and its consequent impacts. In the post-modern literature, the same aspect of decaying railways and a constant throbbing for the reincarnation of railways can be witnessed.

This paper emphasises the importance of the railways in American life and American people. This paper would also try to bring forward the presentation of the railways in the post-modern American literature. The paper also focuses on the key reasons behind the decadence of the American railways in the twentieth century. By doing this, it would also talk about the impacts that the railroads had on the American people in the beginning of the nineteenth century. This paper intends to highlight the change of railways representation in the nineteenth century with the railway representation in the twentieth century literature, particularly in the post-modern period. This paper also focuses on certain issues and aspects which were responsible for the degradation of the railways in the middle half of the twentieth century. This paper, in addition discusses various kinds of representation of the railways in the literary field, specifically after the 1960s.

Before going straight into the discussion about the American railways as represented in the post-modern American literature, it would be worthwhile to talk about the railroads and railway representation in the middle half of the twentieth century or to be specific, in the beginning of the railways in 1830s. Many a nineteenth century prominent writers wrote about their contemporary crucial aspects. And in the nineteenth century, the introduction of railways in the American landscape was a very crucial aspect. And for this reason, there was literature specifically concerning the railways. Many a writers wrote about the impact and importance of the railways in the development of American society and culture. In the poem, "To a Locomotive in Winter," written by Walt Whitman, a true picture of railways in the nineteenth century America could be seen very easily. The poem, first appeared in February 19, 1876, praises railroads in the American landscape. The poem chiefly considers the dynamic relationship between the railroad and nature. The poem transcends railways and made it a part of nature. The essentiality of the railways had been compared with the essentiality of the existence of nature. In fact, the existence of railroads transformed American lives and gave it a proper and dynamic shape.

In the poems of Henry David Thoreau, Emile Dickinson and Emerson, the railways had been given tremendous importance and considered as life and blood for the existence and development of America. Thoreau's "Walden" brought forward the importance of the railroads for the survival and extension of American life and society in the nineteenth century. Thoreau described railways according to its multiple facets. The sound of the railway steam engine and its horn becomes a thing of nature. In the poem "Sounds," Thoreau beautifully amalgamates the railways running sounds with the sound of the kettles and like a thing of wonder and joy, bringing hope, prosperity and tranquility. In the poems of Emile Dickinson, the railways, train and railroads received metaphorical meaning and trains became a symbol of joy, breaking free from the traditional chains, which holds back prosperity and development. In the poem, "I Like to See It Lap the Miles," the railways gets a transcendental and metaphorical meaning. In fact, the nineteenth century American literature glorified and cherished the existence and importance of the railroads for the development and fulfillment of American Dream. Regarding the nineteenth century literature, James C. Bodenstedt comments:

> For many of the 19th century poets, the image of the railroad expresses the promise and the danger of technology in modern industrial society, while the contemporary poets do not generally write poems about the railroad, but use train imagery to journey through the psychic landscape of the century and the one's own mind and being. Today's train poems reveal why they must take a journey through the landscape of the self in order to be fully awake in the world. (2)

In the beginning of the twentieth century, the same sort of phenomenon and energy regarding the railways could be seen in American literature concerning the railroads and railway endeavors. James C. Bodenstedt comments:

> American railroads and American poetry came into the twentieth century on the same track. The railroad revolutionised life and changed the face of the continent. By 1917, our once agrarian nation had evolved as the foremost industrial economy in the world. Track mileage soared. Passenger trains and freight trains increased steadily. The train had tied the nation together in a web of wood and steel and, seemingly, fulfilled Whitman's vision to unite the world in brotherhood. At the same time, poetry had made a radical break from the English tradition and held the promise and hope of Whitman's vision, but American poets of the early century still clung to British continent. (33)

It was a fact that the American railways started to degrade in the beginning of the twentieth century. After the industrial revolution, which was brought about by the introduction of the railways, the railways started to degrade because of the economic development and a number of people denying traveling through trains. The train transport medium devastated because of the economy development, many a people became rich and majority of the American people preferred personal vehicle than trains. Many a people started to put more value on the roads and for this reason the railways, specifically the passenger trains, degraded handsomely. Automobiles came in fashion and a symbol of progress and prestige. The hustle and bustle of city life became the central theme of the literature after the mid-twentieth century.

It needs to be mentioned here that the railways ceased to be the prime transport medium in the early half of the twentieth century, and the impact of war fell heavily on the railways in the beginning of the twentieth century. The war poetry, war novels and several other literary or non-literary texts started to portray railways as the medium of death and bearer of death news. The troop trains and its imagery in the postmodern literature were prominent. Railways, all of a sudden started to be seen as only the medium of transporting goods and troops to the battlefield. The railway in that time was mostly associated with the blood of the soldiers and people trying to escape from a particular place. The refugees and migrants were numerous in numbers. In this way the peaceful existence of the railways shattered. However, it needs to be mentioned that the horrific nature of war was not the only barrier regarding the non-peaceful atmosphere of the railways. In the mid-nineteenth century, many African-Americans tried to escape the wrath of the white Europeans or the white Americans. The racial nature of non-tranquility was also there in the middle half of the nineteenth century. Many novels were based on racial injustice, associated their stories with the trains and railroads. Railroads in those times were the images of freedom and safety. Many Negroes tried to escape by trains and the association of unrest was not something new for the American people. In this aspect James C. Bodenstedt, says: "Langston Hughes is the best poet of the twentieth century to represent the use of the railroad as a symbol of freedom for the African-American spirit.... Yet several of his railroad poems speak of the isolation and oppression of the African-Americans."

But it was a fact that the modern era, that is, the beginning of the twentieth century, was in much trouble and unrest because of the war. The war impacted the growth and continuity of the railways importance in the American lives. The war reduced the amount of money needed to be invested for the development of the railways. The war also reduced the maintenance and damage recovery actions. And for this reason, many a railways ceased its operation in the middle half of the twentieth century, specifically after the 1950s. For this reason, in the literature of the 1960s the imagery of railways changed significantly. At one point the railroads and trains were the carrier of peace and prosperity but later on it ceased its operation almost completely and consequently the imagery of joyfulness changed into the imagery of hopelessness. In the novel *A Farewell to Arms,* Ernest Hemingway depicts railway as a hopeless phenomenon. Railroads and trains were symbolised into an emblem of farewell and something as departure of good times and arrival of a heartless and dark ambience deprived of joyfulness and tranquility. The empty tracks and trains became symbols of a dying generation which was once young and fruitful, filled with vigour and prosperity. In the post-modern period, the once flourishing railways got the imagery of a dying decade and cold death.

The reason behind the degradation of the American railways could be seen in the moves of the parliament and American government to increase the capacity of the roads instead of railways. The American parliament and its wealthy members decided against the railway improvements, they did not saw it necessary for the improvement and betterment of the country. Their focus was on the improvement of roads and increasing it in a rapid speed. Because, according to them, the railways could not bring that amount of profit, specifically in the passenger trains because many a people avoided railways and considered it as a transport medium of the poor and the needy. Even in the transport of goods, trucks started to be getting much more importance than the railways because of its greater efficiency. Trucks were considered and given an upper hand over the railways because trucks were faster than railways in providing door to door service at a tremendous amount of speed and rapidity. For all sorts of reasons, railways were neglected in the mid-twentieth century and several railroads and trains ceased its operation and became rust and scrap irons. It is important to mention here that it was not only the government that hampered progress for the railways, but schemes to increase the use of some routes, or indeed reinstate working on lines, were opposed by well-organised local-interests.

Thus the improvement and renaissance of the railways seemed a difficult task in the post-modern era, where travelling through trains and goods transportation became and less important day by day. In some of the literary pieces in the post-modern period, there had been a picture of emptiness, decay and sadness in the trains and railroads. In many novels and short stories, the departure of trains had been portrayed as departure of joy and departure of some loved ones. The empty station premises and trains signified the emptiness in the human heart in the post-modern American literature. In many American plays of the post-modern era where train imagery or a picture of the railways had been shown, one could find mourning for the lost generation. Several books of the post-modern period portray railways as a medium of uselessness. However, in many of the short stories and novels, the trains had been portrayed as a thing of nostalgia, taking us way back into the growing age of prosperity and peace of American life. Many a trains portray nostalgia and for this reason, many a stories give a slumber account of the past days and recall the days of those times where the Americans used to travel by the trains and enjoyed its importance in the development of American society.

However, in the 1960s, a new urge for the railways started to be coming with a steady pace. The increase in oil price and rising population in the world and also in America, made the by-road travel costly and less preferable. From this period, many a people shifted their choice from personal vehicle to the train transport medium. Because of the price hike of oil and rising population, the Government also started to focus on the importance of the railways in the post-modern period. It needed to be mentioned that, trains would be most suitable and desirable in the upcoming days because of its efficiency and multiple profits. To combat the price hike of oil and other natural resources, which would one day cease to exist, and in that time, the railways would be the utter most important for the transport of passengers and also of goods. To counter the rising population and dense population in a particular place, the railroads became the sole solution. As a result of these apprehensions by the parliament or the Government of America a new focus was given in the 1960s to the railroads. However, the new focus and importance barely helped the railways or the private companies to run the railways, which were left unused for several decades and trains along with the track line had been damaged for no maintenance over several decades.

Amtrak gave a new hope for the bringing back of the glory days of the railways and also to fulfill the nostalgic urge of the twentieth century literature. It was an undeniable truth that, running the existence trains would call for an immediate loss and could harm the railroad on a permanent basis. And since this sort of services were loss making, throwing in their lot with Amtrak seemed the least bad option. In the initial moments of the post-modern days, particularly in the 1960s, it was decided that the railroads would supply crews to operate trains, but the on-board staff such as catering staff and porters were to be Amtrak employees. It was, as George H. Douglas puts it, 'a typically American compromise – the kind of thing that makes no one totally happy.' To move from the city bustle, people again opted for the railways, which ran across woods and grass fields and in the natural settings of the most important nature.

The post-modern nostalgia for the railways seemed to be too important for the peace and comfort of the American people and also for bringing back the same amount of impetus and vigour of the early nineteenth century. It is needed to be mentioned here that Amtrak was introduced for the reincarnation of the lost days of the railways but it failed to achieve the desired results. It is also pertinent to mention here that Amtrak's network was 'just a skeleton of a skeleton' as so many services had already been closed down by the private railroads with the permission of the Interstate Commerce Commission and Amtrak was not even in a position to run all the promised routes on day one. Jim MaClellan, the key official in the railroad division of the Department of Transportation, admitted that promoting Amtrak as a convention profit seeking company was a great deception and yet absolutely necessary to win over the politicians the idea: 'We did not put all our cards on the table. We bent the truth. That's politics.' Amtrak was very much profitable because of its cheaper cost of fare and goods transportation. And in this aspect Richard Saunders Jr. commented that, "For the first time, cattle in large numbers could be raised and fattened on cheap western grain in the mild climate of the South."

In the 1970s freight trains were the backbones of American railways and the majority of the trains that were running on the tracks were the goods trains. There was less number of passenger trains. Many a states and districts of America did not have passenger trains running on the tracks, even if there were trains, those trains were not frequent in numbers and most of them only ran on the weekends and holidays or on specific dates. The introduction of the airways also ended the railway journey craze among the American people, because the airway travels were faster than the railway travelling and people had less time for things and specifically for journey in the 1970s. It is important to mention here that Amtrak did not always live up to its first slogan, 'We are making the trains worth traveling again'. In the early days its trains were run in all kinds of random liveries and in such a poor condition that at one point in the mid-1970 'these rolling junk boxes were catching fire at the rate of one a day.'

All sorts of peculiar conditions were there in the development of the railways in the 1970s. To give rebirth to the dying age of railways, a number of initiatives were taken in the post-modern period but majority of them failed to achieve the desired results. Apparently, it was a fact that, the lost generation of the good old days of railways in America could never be brought back because of such peculiar circumstances in the railway management and development process. And in the post-modern days, alternatives of the passenger trains became a prominent aspect. Speed trains, trims, metro rails started to occupy the centre stage in the fast-forward post-modern days where everything happens very quickly and everything needs to be on time. The time efficiency had been the prominent reason behind the reincarnation of rails through the alternatives. And it had been a fact that metros and speed trains for long distance journeys became prominent and gets more preference than any other ways. Traveling airways had been costly and many citizens could not afford to travel by airways. For all such reasons, along with petroleum price hike and rising population, railroads seemed to be the only solution for such auspicious circumstances.

All such aspects of railways get beautifully delineated in an artistic manner in the literary works and representations. The industrial revolution and rapidity of life gets efficiently described in the novels, short stories and poems of several authors. It is also pertinent to mention here that many stories take us back to the early nineteenth century and give us a feeling of nostalgia and a hope of rebirth of the dying generation. In the short stories of A. E. Poe, the mention of the railways gets a touch of horror and a somber atmosphere, imagery of trains running across the untrodden wood in the dark night under the moony sky. Imagery of death and restlessness, fatality, hopelessness, nostalgia, sympathy, desire for a railway renaissance and a bringer of tranquility in the modern days of haste and restlessness, had been the major train and railway imageries of the twentieth century or specifically of the post-modern period. However, it is important to mention here that the railways of the post-modern period started to witness an upsurge in existence and emergence of a newly modified version of railway infrastructure and maintenance for the continuance of a age old glorious tradition of running trains in the mighty landscape of America.

To conclude the findings about the existence of the railways in the post-modern days, specifically in the literature of the post-modern days, we could say that the railways had lost the glory and vigor of the early nineteenth century and had found itself amidst a mess. There had been an obvious shift in the representation of the railways in the nineteenth century American literature with the post-modern representation of American railways in literature. In the early nineteenth century, trains and railroads had been associated with joy, peacefulness, a thing of nature, carrier of prosperity and development, messenger of hope and many other positive aspects. But the after decades of world wars, specifically the era of 1960 onwards, the representation of the age old imagery of railways changed significantly in the context meaning and became a symbol of hopelessness and emptiness. Post-modern writers such as, Thomas Pynchon, John Barth, Don Delillo, Paul Auster, used railways less significantly and most of the imageries of railways represented failure, hopelessness, nostalgia, despair, melancholy, emptiness. Though there had been images of railway rebirth and the railway renaissance bringing about joy and peacefulness into the minds and hearts of the depressed American souls of the post-modern era, the post-modern American literature chiefly hints at the dyeing generation of railways, which was once filled with joy, vigour, enthusiasm, tranquility and prosperity.

Works Cited

Bodenstedt, James C. "The Railroad in American Poetry". *English Master's Theses. Digital Commons.* digitalcommons.brockport.edu/eng_theses/120. Accessed 12 March 2021.

Douglas, George H. *All Aboard: The Railroad in American Life.* Paragon House, 1992.

Saunders Jr., Richard. *Merging Lines: American Railroads, 1900-1970.* Northern Illinois UP, 2001.

CHAPTER 7

Self-Reflexivity in the Select Novels of Paul Auster

J. Iswarya

Contemporary American literature is largely a consequence of plentiful number of influences, both external and internal, experienced over a period of almost four centuries, starting from the Renaissance movement in Europe. American literature has seen sensational growth in terms of experimentation since the modern period. Writers have engineered fresh forms for their content, and have employed innovative styles to deliver it, relentlessly reinvigorating how an American novel can be. Labels such as modern, post-modern, post-structuralist, and even post-post-modern have cropped up to categorise their works. Experimental fiction has always been interesting in spite of their demanding techniques and unintelligible styles. During the modernist period, social conflicts and familial issues had superior importance, and alienation, disillusionment and frustration became the catchphrases of literature. Realism slowly gave way to existential dilemma aptly symbolised by open-ended structures, defying all the genre-conventions. Roughly, the novel since 1945 has been called 'postmodern'. However, this random demarcation is of little value, taking into account the nature of the postmodern novel that inherently refuses to give in to any such classification.

Postmodern writers share the same skepticism of the modernist authors who wrote in the first few decades of the twentieth century, but with one major difference: while the modernist felt a terrible sense of failure looking for 'meaning' in 'the grand narratives', in vain; the postmodernists delight in the dissolution of those established 'grand narratives', which, according to them, ordained single truth, distinct meaning, sole essence – a position which was absolutely deplorable to their predecessors. Postmodern literature, which is inherently self-reflexive in nature, glorifies the battles fought by the writer and discusses his journey as a 'writer' at length.

Postmodern literary criticism rejects the notion that literary texts have objective meanings and true interpretations. All such claims to objectivity and truth can be deconstructed. (Hicks 16) As the centre shifts from the writer to the reader, the reader holds supreme authority over the work of fiction at hand. To retain his power and position, to establish his original autonomy over his creation, the writer begins to explain his craft to his readers. This is, indeed, paradoxical because to gain his power, he has to first lose it. He must forget it. His narration more or less focuses entirely on the art of narration, thereby exposing the self-conscious nature of the work to his readers. This came to be known as 'metafiction', where the writer lays his work bare in front of his readers' eyes – allowing them to participate in the making itself.

In his works, Paul Auster, a contemporary American writer, personifies his own character that is torn between the randomness of the massive stretch of his country and the complexity of his inner self that strains to make sense of its existence. The ghosts of the past haunt him not just from the outside. He has to fight with them from within. His protagonists are all impatient men on quests who thirst for the impeccable knowledge of their identity, going through inexplicable patterns that often mislead them beyond imagination, bestowing upon them with nothing but the experience of it. This experience and awareness make them lose their innocence and going one step further, lose their identity, taking them farther away from their goal. The postmodern potpourri makes them lose their faces, purpose and even their souls.

Surviving the Postmodern condition is not only gradually more challenging but also extremely exigent for Paul Auster, the writer. His technique and style are impregnated with modern thoughts, ideas and philosophies but he ensures that he is unique in his own way by layering them within a labyrinth of postmodern sensibilities. This explains why Auster's characters resemble one another and Auster himself and yet how they are so dissimilar by nature. That is, besides creating a fictional world, the writer (who is the hero) also invents characters to inhabit the world. The multiple selves are created purposefully in the image of the writer's self as he is no longer satisfied with the externalised journey of the physical. He hungers to conduct his Self on a journey to a higher Self that is primarily psychological and pragmatically spiritual.

Hence, Auster, as the hero, chooses 'metafiction' as the mode of journey through space, a journey from the Self to reach the Self. This journey tends to be vertical. This is allegorically presented by the way of a narrative style that rejects grand narratives, faithfully adhering to Lyotard's theory. Though the narration is seemingly linear, it also has a ghost that transports it to the past and a shadow that propels it forward. The Self is, however, aware of the development, as it progresses on its quest, that it constantly refers to itself to the extent of narcissism, obsessed with the idea of its own Self, thereby considerably using the 'metafictional' technique propounded by Patricia Waugh and acknowledging its own status as a text.

Postmodern literature can be described as the literature of the Self, only that its approach is vastly different from the literatures of the earlier periods. In *A Poetic of Postmodernism: History, Theory, Fiction* (1988), Hutcheon observes that postmodern literature makes use of a language of decentering rather than the language of alienation as it was arbitrary before, "because the center used to function as the pivot between binary opposites which always privileged one half: white/ black, male/female, self/other, intellect/body, west/east, objectivity/ subjectivity – the list is now well known" (62). Hence, the postmodern identity is formed not based entirely on a subjective analysis of the Self, alienating the Other, but by approaching the Self from the Other, where both these terms are capriciously interchangeable.

To explain this, Hutcheon alludes to Lacanian ideology that calls for the consideration of the 'object' (the Other) – as a function within a symbolic order, as structured by language as difference, instead of as a unified autonomous consciousness (169). Lacan clinically fuses the Freudian concept of identity with structuralism from a Derrida's deconstructive perspective by asserting that meaning can be created only by differences and sustained only by reference to other meaning. Thus, difference is the very basis of the Lacanian definition of the split subject as a meaning producing entity, itself constructed from a system of differences (65).

Lacan describes the "mirror-stage" as an important step towards establishing a "relation between the organism and its reality" (Ragupathi 4). Lacan feels the urge to distinguish between need, demand and desire. According to him, need belongs to the realm of the Real. All the basic needs for survival of mankind come under this realm and are easily satisfied. However, demand belongs to the realm of the Imaginary. It is subtle response to the other which is imaginary by nature. Whereas, desire belongs to the realm of the Symbolic that is it can never be satiable and is always discontented. The Subject always desires the Other and that is why, Auster's characters incessantly exasperate to take hold of the otherness and strive to seek its reflection in themselves. It is the insatiable hunger with which his heroes walk the roads of consciousness.

Thus, with Daniel Quinn (the protagonist of *City of Glass)*, Auster gives form to his alter-ego and allows him to meet Paul Auster, a sadder fictional version of himself, in an alternative universe where he has no family. He sees himself in both Quinn and Paul Auster, but the fact is, the entirely fictional Quinn resembles him more than the partially fictional Auster. Clearly, Auster asserts his idea that the Other can easily flow into the Self, just as a reflection of the subject swaps the subject itself.

Daniel Quinn is not a random name given to a random character. The starting letters of the first and the last names are reminiscent of the Spanish adventurous hero Don Quixote of La Mancha. Peter Stillman is also not an arbitrary name. There has been a contemporary writer of Myth criticism who shares his name with him. Auster gives the same name Peter Stillman to both the father and, and the son, to the hunter and the hunted, to the two diagonally opposite characters in a move to show how the son inherits everything from his father, even though they have nothing in common except the name. None can ignore the ease with which Daniel Quinn flows into the mask of William Wilson, Max Work and Paul Auster himself.

Virginia Dare was the name of the first English baby born in the New World; precisely the reason why the name is more popular in America than elsewhere. The baby was named after the Colony of Virginia, which was itself named for Elizabeth I, the Virgin Queen. The name became common in the 19th century. Hence, Auster names the only female character in *City of Glass* as Virginia, trying to revivify the great American tradition and its historical significance.

Additionally, Auster himself is a writer like Quinn who is quite shy to reveal his true personality that he does not entertain readers or fans in his company very easily. He does all his communications through his agent and confines them all to mail. Only recently does he appear in public very often. Otherwise, he likes to keep to himself. Moreover, the idea of inheritance from which Quinn says that he manages to live is something Auster repeats in many of his subsequent novels.

The second book *Ghosts* does not guarantee the kind of irony that one is exposed to in the first book of the Trilogy. Here, everything is made explicit. The self-referentiality is overtly obvious as the action starts on Auster's birthday, that on 3rd February 1947. Even though, Black and Blue are introduced to the readers as two different characters, after a while, the bartering takes place so painlessly, that the reader imagines Blue when he reads about Black and vice versa. When Blue is the subject, Black is the reflected image, and when Black is the subject Blue becomes his faithful image. What makes the experience both perplexing and exciting is that the conventional roles of a hard-boiled detective fiction – that of a detective and his prime subject, pour into each other in the most unconventional way possible.

Though it is evident even from the beginning that Black and Blue bear an unnatural, creepy resemblance to each other in the way they appear and do things, it is only from the point of view of Blue that the reader gets the drift of everything happening. But what makes this novel essentially gripping is that, even as the story seems to be moving, it actually remains the same from the beginning till the end. Nothing really happens in the pages of the book, except the empty rumblings of Blue revealing his suspicions and horrors. Intermittently, the narrator intervenes with his observations and comments.

When Elisabeth M. Loevlie in her article, "Faith in the Ghosts of Literature – Poetic Hauntology in Derrida, Blanchot and Morrison's *Beloved*" argues that "The "I" that speaks in a literary text never coincides with the "I" of the writing subject, rather they haunt each other" (336), basing her argument on the findings of Jacques Derrida and Maurice Blanchot, she attempts to describe the concept of hauntology in literature. She calls attention to that attribute of literature that can transmit the ineffable, the repressed and transcendent, making it superior to history in every possible way. She contends:

> To live is to be haunted. Our "here and now", our material presence, is never stripped, bare or alone. Neither is our subjectivity. We are always caught up in invisible and intangible webs of the past, of the other, of the future, of death. Our existence is therefore always *in-between*, defined of course by the materiality of our present being, but also by this immaterial flux that surrounds and situates us. (337)

In keeping with what Loevlie maintains, what fill the pages of this book are chiefly the ghosts of the writer's past. Auster uses Blue's childhood memories to give vent to his knowledge of the history of the Brooklyn Bridge. There are several instances where Auster rather exploits Blue to speak about his literary ancestors like Thoreau, Whitman and Hawthorne. However, he makes sure that they blend with the flow of narration as he places them alongside Blue's father, an absent figure who haunts Blue just as those dead literary figures.

Blue tells himself, "This isn't the story of my life, after all" and he reassures himself saying, "I'm supposed to be writing about him, not myself" (175). Blue even confesses to himself that "he is developing a certain fondness for Black" (181), expressing the love for his object of investigation. Like Blue, Black also maintains a notebook where he records things which the former has no idea of. However, with no logical explanation whatsoever, he decides to buy a copy of Henry David Thoreau's *Walden* (1854) and only states, "If he can't read what Black writes, at least he can read what he reads." (181). A long shot, as Blue himself admits, he goes ahead with the hope that it will "give some hint of what the man is up to" (181).

The unnamed narrator of the third book of the Trilogy, *The Locked Room* follows the well-trodden path of Quinn and Blue as he identifies himself with his childhood friend, Fanshawe straightaway. The opening lines of the novel show how his identity is inseparable from that of Fanshawe: "It seems to me now that Fanshawe was always there. He is the place where everything begins for me, and without him I would hardly know who I am." Gonsalez, in his essay, "Subterranean Autobiographies: *The 'Solitude Trilogy'* Versus *The New York Trilogy*" observes that Auster extends Lacan's idea of the mirror stage to self-consciousness and self-observation in adulthood as a means of acquiring identity and forming our own personality (81).

Once again, Auster proves to be a conformed narcissist as he deliberately gives away all his biographical details in the act of creating the narrator who is assigned no name and his doppelganger, Fanshawe. Fanshawe, like Auster is a writer based in New York, born in February 1947. His wife Sophie is of Norwegian origin just like his wife. As an extraordinary case, Auster has named his daughter 'Sophie' after this character. Like Auster's mother, Fanshawe's also lives in New Jersey and he too has a son and a neurotic sister. All that Fanshawe likes stem from Auster's own likings and the problems he faces as a youngster are directly lifted from the episodes in Auster's life. Like some of the other Auster heroes, Fanshawe spends a considerable part of his writing life in Paris and takes up translating and teaching jobs. Auster does not even miss the interest that he had in movies and the small-time odd jobs that he did to make his ends meet. Auster toys with the idea of 'What if' once again with Fanshawe's character. While the fictional character of Paul Auster in *City of Glass*, discusses about the probability of Auster's success if he had not met Siri, *The Locked Room* visualises a Paul Auster who becomes a 'nobody' just like the invisible Fanshawe who has no identity without his works.

The narrator of *The Locked Room* is not given a name intentionally because he is, for all intents and purposes, a man without a face. He is merely a reflection, an image without a body of his own. When the reader is getting used to the idea of the swapping of masks, Auster surprises him by introducing him to the idea of swapping faces. Without a name, the narrator becomes a faceless personality and it becomes easier for the reader to accept him as Fanshawe's double. Whatever the reader knows of Fanshawe is only from the words of the narrator; so as he constructs the character of Fanshawe, he constructs his own character too.

Being Fanshawe's childhood friend, it is not difficult for the reader to visualise and recognise the narrator as a man born in the same month and year. Auster assigns some of the roles taken up by him in the course of his life even to the narrator and sees him as his double just like Fanshawe. That is, Auster identifies himself with Fanshawe as well as with the unnamed narrator, just like how the narrator identifies himself with his friend.

The inability of the characters to distinguish reality from illusion is the direct outcome of the writer's inability to differentiate his memories from his dreams and fantasies. The Self of the writer tries to tread the treacherous path of the psyche with limited estimation of truth and uses the realm of fiction to explore the enigmas of his identity. As the Self enters the territory of the Other, it becomes the Other and thus, the Self of the writer is realised in the Self of the protagonist, as the reader becomes the inevitable Other who gives meaning to the otherwise deplorable text that symbolises the innermost quandaries of the mind. In Auster's novel, the geographical space of the city is also closely linked with the Self inhabiting it.

All these works are but literature about literature no more than that Quinn's case is Stillman's, which in turn is Henry Dark's, Blue's case is Black's, the narrator's is Fanshawe's. Frederic Jameson calls attention to the fact that the postmodern schizophrenic selves are "capable of modifying their shapes so effectively that they ultimately call the very idea of the self into question" (189). He calls for an alternate reading according to which the self is constituted like private property, or even on the model of private property that resonates across some very different zones of modern thought, above all in those areas where the ego or personal identity has been the most strongly experienced as an unstable construction (199).

Paul Auster's fiction can be called by several names including factional writing, autobiographical fiction, confessional writing and so on. He conceives his Self as being passive, presenting it from an objective point of view. The incidents and experiences from his life are presented analytically with clinical perfection. The turmoil of the psychosomatic state of affairs becomes the terrain from which he delivers his chaotic art that indulges deeply in the obsession with the personal facts. To him, writing is an intimate exercise, a penance that will eventually lead to his personal redemption – an atonement that is the desperate need of any postmodern writer of his generation. His literature is a dramatisation of the Self, where he places it in focus with itself. The strong autobiographical element that runs in his works is not accidental. It is an attempt of an individual to universalise his personal identity crisis through his words.

Giddens mentions that in the postmodern world, an individual struggles to assert his true self because, the "false self-overrides and blankets out the original acts of thinking, feeling and willing which represent the true motivations of the individual. What remains of the true self is experienced as empty and inauthentic" (418). When he speaks of the difference between the Self in the traditional world and that in the more extensive modern world (which can be even more proper for the Self in the postmodern world), he recalls the précis of Marx's principles: "In contrast to the traditional world, it is supposed, where the individual was substantially in control of many of the influences shaping his life, in modern societies that control has passed to external agencies" (419).

Reading Auster's postmodern fiction, one may essentially come to the conclusion that the identity of the writer is formed based on his parentage, background, nationality, past, memories, his personal likes and dislikes, his society, his race, his contemporaries and several other factors which have an eternal impact on him. Therefore, the Self of the writer is not a singular unified phenomenon. It is multiple and diversified. It is something that is dynamic in nature and keeps evolving in the process.

Works Cited

Auster, Paul. *The New York Trilogy*. Penguin, 1990.

Godden's, Anthony. "Modernity and Self-identity: Tribulations of the Self." *The Discourse Reader,* edited by Adam Jaworski and Nikolas Coupland. Routledge, 1999, pp. 415-27.

Gonsalez, Jesus Angel. "Subterranean Autobiographies: The 'Solitude' Trilogy versus The New York Trilogy." *Critical Engagements: A Journal of Criticism and Theory,* vol.7 no.1, 2013, pp. 71-88.

Hicks, Stephen Ronald Craig. *Explaining Postmodernisn: Skepticism and Socialism from Rousseau to Foucault.* Scholarly Pub., 2004.

Hutcheon, Linda. *A Poetics of Postmodernism: History, Theory, Fiction.* Routledge, 1988.

Loevlie, Elisabeth M. "Faith in the Ghosts of Literature. Poetic Hauntology in Derrida, Blanchot and Morrison's *Beloved.*" *Religions,* vol. 4, no.3, 2013, pp. 336-50.

Ragupathi, K. V. "Beyond Theory." *Literary Theories in Application,* edited by Sunita Jakhar, Aadi Publications, 2010, pp. 3-12.

CHAPTER 8

An Intrinsic Insight into the Contemporary Post-Modern Literary Image of 'Hyperrealism' in the Lens of David Foster Wallace

Aditi Abhishikta

Foster Wallace unfurled the datum intact that the fictions produced in the early 1990s by the American authors gave birth to a new genus of fiction, and bidden to explicate the footings on which that narrative was recounting. In the following times, a good collection of authors and reviewers have progressively acknowledged that there has indeed been the existence of a kind of profound high post modernism imprint in many of the remarkable and appealingly efficacious productions by the geniuses like Thomas Pynchon, John Barth and Robert Coover in their narratives.

Likewise, efforts have been put by many to label the outline of this alteration and elucidate the essential foundations of the squabble being stirredupon. Through in most of the exemplary grounds, these efforts determine that fictionsat contemporary times propose an expansion of or redeploying on some of the derelict facets of postmodernist literature. In some of the works such as Jeremy Green's 2005 *Late Postmodernism: American Fiction at the Millennium* and *or, The Cultural Logic of Just-in-Time Capitalism*, by Jeffrey T. Nealon in 2012 for instance, infer the notion of 'late postmodernist' or 'post-postmodernist' narratives as mark of escalation of the influence of late capitalist economies and microelectronic intervention on ethnic making. In some other works such as the writers of the essays in Alison Shonkwiler and Leigh Clare La Berge's 2012 *Reading Capitalist Realism* and James Wood (albeit less flatteringly) in his 2000 review 'Human, all too Inhuman,' advocates that narrative is, triggered by several of those similar elements, experiencing an intransigent return to Realist aesthetics.

Conversely, several critics claim for a rather more far-reaching break between the postmodern and post-postmodern, as Alan Kirby in his 2009 *Digimodernism: How New Technologies Dismantle the Postmodern and Reconfigure Our Culture* has exemplified. Despite of some differences among the critics concerning the nature and notch of difference between the postmodern and the post-postmodern, there exists a broad reception of the impression that claims like Foster Wallace's are on the dent in the realm of contemporary American fiction has, since coarsely 1989, progressively valorised such apparently naïve fictitious potentials as a reappearance to imitative credibility, a spectacle of historical consciousness, and a concern with the somatic nature of the documented artifact as means to the renaissance of a productive verbatim legitimacy, the one which revives the interchange between reader and literary text.

Though the above-mentioned sections arise only in 2005, their signatures are felt even before during the 1990s and early 2000s that designate a deeper wide spread past of rational thought with regard to the substance. Prominent exemplary pieces such as Heide Ziegler's symposium 'The End of Postmodernism' in 1991, Mark Amerika and Lance Olsen's urgings in *In Memoriam to Postmodernism* (1995) which states that an 'Avant-Pop' artistic has supplanted the postmodernist realm. Distinguished papers are apparently taken into account like Stephen Burn's 'The End of Postmodernism: American Fiction of the Millennium,' the essay in 2000 and Robert McLaughlin's 2004 article 'Post-Postmodern Discontent: Contemporary Fiction and the Social World.' And Raymond Federman's assertion in 2001 that postmodernism perished in 1989, with the bereavement of Samuel Beckett. In the stream of ascertaining the changing nature of a post-postmodern turn, there residues substantial incongruity among critics concerning a right number of aspects connected to the classification and narrative of any of the contemporary expansions in fiction.

Moreover, the terms like 'post-postmodernist,' 'Avant-Pop,' 'dig modernist,' and 'New Sincerity' is identified to be margined in certain rooms as deficient. One intrusion made by the insightful critics and writers in this concern has been their proposition of using the articulation of 'met modernism' as a term appropriate enough to both the transferal in fictitious exercise and all of the numerous abilities and trepidations that has been offered to describe the shift. One of the best proclamations of this locus so far is Robin van den Akker, Alison Gibbons, and Timotheus Vermeulen's collection *Metamodernism: Historicity, Affect, and Depth after Postmodernism* in 2017. The term 'metamodernism' assumes to occupy a comprehensible marker next to postmodernism, thereby welcoming enquiries regarding the post-postmodern turn's features and inferences that are hardly determined. Undeniably, the sequences of the former passages signpost the noteworthy intensity to which this critical deliberation involving the post-postmodern appears to be fragmentary challenging. In the epilogue to *The Politics of Postmodernism*, 2002, Linda Hutcheon proposes that absence of lucidity is an issue of immense alarm, because the incapability to institute the lexicon and broad drive of intricate ventures involving contemporary fictional energies obstructs not just the intricate creativity, but the diffusion of intricate insights to a broader interview. The studies poised in this concern of *Textual Practice* originated with an acknowledgment that urgings and inquisitiveness on what trails postmodernism have established within a few of steadyloci. And the study demands a fresh overview on emerging texts and arguments with the special issue of *Twentieth Century Literature* on a parallel strand.

Andrew Hoberek (ed.), *Twentieth Century Literature*, special issue: After Postmodernism: Form and History in Contemporary Fiction, (Fall 2007), touches upon several conversant facts and methodologies, the collectively amplified inferences of the continuing conversation about post-postmodernist American literature as discovered in many of its conclusive texts. Here an attempt has been made to outline an ephemeral impression of these contexts.

In 1961 Philip Roth wrote an essay 'Writing American Fiction' which very much triggers the present context and throws light on how "the serious writer' has failed to find an appropriate strategy or form for dealing with the reality of the social and historical world.' With the issue diagnosed by Philip Roth there might be two possible solutions offered in American writing, one, that produced 'New Journalism' and that of the 'Non-Fiction Novel'. The writers with regard to these forms such as Tom Wolfe and Truman Capote operated the skills of fiction in a challenge to achieve a grander point of credibility. In the eyes of Wolfe such narrative 'enjoys an advantage so obvious, so built in, one almost forgets what a power it has [...] the simple fact that the reader knows all this actually happened. The disclaimers are erased. The screen is gone. The writer is one step closer to the absolute involvement of the reader that Henry James and James Joyce dreamed of and never achieved.' In the arguments of Capote, such form 'remove disguises,' from the exemplification of the 'social and historical world,' and substantiates the ground that let the realities ostensibly voice for themselves. The writers of Postmodernism have taken the reverse stand. As Barth has rightly remarked, 'A different way to come to terms with the discrepancy between art and the Real Thing is to affirm the artificial element in art (you can't get rid of it anyhow) and make the artifice part of your point.' This, evidently, is the ideology of the meta-fictionists, and it is originated from the proposition delineated by Ronald Sukenick that 'reality is, simply, our experience and objectivity is, of course, an illusion.'

'The Babysitter' by Coover disturbed the discrepancy that has arisen between 'objective' reality and experience, by repudiating to differentiate between what really happens, what the characters are willing to happen and what might conceivably happen. Coover institutes a chronicle world where the common concords and television apparently appears to have created and directed the characters' comportment. Ronald Christ states that destabilising the difference between artifice, fantasy, and reality assumes that everything that is read in the story needs to be observed as 'both true and false, as both happening and not happening.' This 'illusion' of detachment or impartiality is also observed in the work of E. L. Doctorow during the 1970s and 1980s and directed him to relinquish what he termed as the 'chaste or objective voice of realism.' Doctorow further suggested, in one of his important essays 'False Documents,' that 'there is no fiction or non-fiction as we commonly understand the distinction: there is only narrative,' a theme illustrated in his novel, *Ragtime* (1975), where one sees historical personages 'Harry Houdini, Sigmund Freud, Stanford White' mingling with characters from Doctorow's imagination. While the New Journalism attempted to bring the practices of fiction to the authenticating of the 'real,' the methods observed by Doctorow was to carry the 'real' into his narratives, over meta-fictional expedients, experiment the means of all kinds in which one paradigms the belief of the 'real.' As a matter of fact, it was over such meta-fictional implications that tales might, in sagacity, be transferred: 'It is a world born for liars,' he remarked, 'and we [fiction writers] are born liars. But we are to be trusted because it is the only profession forced to admit that it lies – and it bestows upon us the mantle of honesty.'

According to Robert Rebein, during 1980s there was also a trace of American writing which evaded such implications giving emphasis upon 'revitalisation of realism.' Before Rebeinproposed his squabble in the book *Hicks, Tribes and Dirty Realists* (2001), the critic James Wood, pioneered in his work, the *New Republic*, by devising the judgmental term 'Hysterical Realism' that would designate both the latest exertion of postmodernists belonging to first-generation such as Pynchon and Don DeLillo, and also the exertion of trending class of writers, like Foster Wallace and Zadie Smith. Foster Wallace's inscription has been seen as the spearhead of an embryonic 'New Sincerity' in American writing.

This writing has included the works of Jennifer Egan, Rick Moody, George Saunders, and Jonathan Franzen, which is largely seen as a challenge to travel yonder the sarcasm of postmodernist narrative, and to hostage the 'waning of affect' that these kinds of fictions effected. The short story 'Octet,' written by Foster Wallace from *Brief Interview with Hideous Men* (1999), has been regarded as the 'Ur-text of New Sincerity.' 'Octet' is offered as a story 'or really a failed story' anxious with attaining compassion and communal with the readers who read; it is the exciting meta-functionality of the script, the way the postmodern narration styles have been worked, and the profuse lengthy footnotes which intend to shoulder the apparent central text, seems to validate how challenging it is to discharge the system of sarcasm and wit that postmodernism mounted. In other words, 'Octet' determines the struggle not in the mirror of being sincere, but of substantiating others of one's sincerity. Here the story concludes by laying its providence in the minds of the reader: 'So decide,' it concludes.

The importance of the datum that critics are at the commencement the chore of delineating inclinations within neorealism is that it appears with the implicit acceptance that the pragmatist turn needs to now be taken for contracted.

Works Cited

Akker, Robin Van Den, et al., editors. *Metamodernism: Historicity, Affect, and Depth after Postmodernism.* Rowman and Littlefield, 2017.

Burn, Stephen. "The End of Postmodernism: American Fiction of the Millennium". *American Fiction of the 1990s: Reflections of history and culture*, edited by Jay Prosser, Routledge, 2000, pp. 220-234.

Capote, Truman. *Music for Chameleons.* Penguin, 1993.

Christ, Ronald. "Forking Narratives". *Latin American Literary Review*, vol. 7, no. 14, 1979, pp. 52-61.

Coover, Robert. "The Babysitter". *Pricksongs and Descants.* Grove, 2000, p. 206-39.

Doctorow, E. L. "'False Documents' 1977". *E. L. Doctorow: Essays and Conversations,* edited by Richard Trenner, Ontario Review P, 1983, pp. 24-26.

Dowling, David. "Raymond Federman's America: Take It or Leave It." *Contemporary Literature*, vol. 30, no. 3, 1989, pp. 348–69. *JSTOR*, www.jstor.org/stable/1208409. Accessed 10 Feb. 2021.

Enck, John J. and John Barth. "John Barth: An Interview", *Contemporary Literature*, vol. 6, no. 1, Winter-Spring 1965, pp. 3-14.

Green, Jeremy. *Late Post Modernism: American Fiction at the Millennium.* Palgrave Macmillan, 2005.

Hoberek, Andrew. "Introduction: After Postmodernism." *Twentieth Century Literature*, vol. 53, no. 3, 2007, pp. 233–247. *JSTOR*, www.jstor.org/stable/20479812. Accessed 10 Feb. 2021.

Hutcheon, Linda. *A Poetics of Postmodernism: History, Theory, Fiction.* Routledge, 1988.

Kelly, Adam. "David Foster Wallace and the New Sincerity in American Fiction." *Consider David Foster Wallace: Critical Essays*, edited by David Hering Sideshow, Media Group Press, 2010, pp. 131-46.

Kirby, Alan. *Digimodernism: How New Technologies Dismantle the Postmodern and Reconfigure Our Culture.* Continuum, 2009.

McLaughlin, Robert L. "Post-Postmodern Discontent: Contemporary Fiction and the Social World." *Symploke*, vol. 12, no. 1/2, 2004, pp. 53-68. *JSTOR*, www.jstor.org/stable/40550666. Accessed 10 Feb. 2021.

Nealon, Jeffery. *The Cultural Logic of Just-in-Time Capitalism.* Stanford UP, 2012.

Olsen, Lance & Mark America, editors. *In Memoriam to Postmodernism.* San Diego State UP, 1995.

Robert Rebein, Hicks, *Tribes and Dirty Realists: American Fiction after Postmodernism.* The UP of Kentucky, 2001, pp. 17-29.

Shonkwiler, Alison, and Berge Leigh Claire La, editors. *Reading Capitalist Realism.* Stanford UP, 2012.

Sukenick, Ronald. 'The Death of the Novel'. *The Death of the Novel and Other Stories.* Fiction Collective 2, 2003, p. 41.

Wallace, David Foster. *Brief Interviews with Hideous Men.* Abacus, 2011.

Wolfe, Tom. "The New Journalism." *The New Journalism,* edited by Tom Wolfe and E. W. Johnson, Picador, 1996, p. 49.

Wood, James. "Human, All Too Inhuman." *The New Republic.* July 24, 2000. newrepublic.com/article/61361/human-inhuman.

Ziegler, Heide. "The End of Postmodernism: New Directions: Proceedings of the First Stuttgart Seminar in Cultural Studies." 04.0.8-18.08.1991.

CHAPTER 9

Predicament of Black Women: Racism and Abusein Alice Walker's *The Colour Purple* and Toni Morrison's *The Bluest Eye*

Anshuman

I

> "It is not our differences that divide us. It is our inability to recognise, accept, and celebrate those differences."
>
> – Audre Lorde

Prevalent since colonial era, racism in America emerged as a practice to differentiate particular groups based on their race and ethnicity. African Americans, probably known to be the descendants of enslaved black people are one of the largest ethnic groups of America. Racism, oppression, subjugation and discrimination done on racial basis to African Americans is itself an evidence of America's dark past and deeds. Belittling and degradation of whole of African American populace on the basis of their skin color and features and superiority of white skin has fetched innumerable atrocities on these people. The denial of basic human rights, inhumane behaviour, mass genocide and forced removals of these people from white land has yielded much criticism and stigma to the perpetrators. Even in 21st century, the outrage spread against killing of many innocent black people has created chaos across the country. Ranging from incidents like killing of police officer, George Floyd in Minnesota to the raised protests namely 'Black Lives Matter' done worldwide shows the torture and brutality on black people. The experiences of African American black women are worse as they face misery based on color and gender. As Simien asserts, "Having to bear the burdens of prejudice that challenge people of color, in addition to the various forms of subjugation that hinder women, African American women are disadvantaged doubly in the social, economic, and political structure of the United States" (83).

African American literature has explored and investigated recurring sociological, political and historical themes, all of which reflect the politics of black experiences. American literature has plethora of works exclusively devoted to the racial discrimination, slavery and experience of black people. Critiquing the racial discourse worldwide, many writers have repeatedly criticized the institution of racial differentiation and the supremacy of white over black in terms of color, intelligence, power and, especially beauty. Utmost contribution to African American literature was done by Phillis Wheatley, the first ever African American woman poet in 1773. Though with passing times many female writers drifted out of their cocoons and expressed the atrocities faced by them due to their race and sex which is valuable. Toni Morrison, Gloria Naylor, Natozaka Shange, Nella Larson, Audre Lorde, Alice Childress, Toni Cade Bambara and Alice Walker are few names who introduced the ignored, misrepresented and mistreated women in literature. They not only created awareness about their experiences but created a revolution also through their marvelous works and nurtured the American literature.

Nobel laureate, Toni Morrison and winner of Pulitzer Prize and National Book Award for fiction, Alice Walker are from the few handful of writers who have not limited their works only to experiences of black men rather they moved forward and explored the less talked about experiences of black women, their exploitation by white men, women and black men as well. Their contribution to African American literature is much appreciable as they restlessly worked for the upliftment of the black women. Both the writers have incorporated the experiences of victims of racial discrimination, abuse, gender biasness, rapes, slavery, oppression, domination and exploitations may it be physical, psychological or emotional.

II

Female oppression and exploitation have always been an issue of debate though women of all races, religions and cultures experience various kinds of oppression and discrimination but black women's oppression differs from white ones. Rigid political and social structure, discriminatory patriarchal norms and taboos largely affected the African

American women since centuries. Undergoing double oppression, based on gender, race, prejudice and misogynistic interpretations the experiences of black women in history are touching and sombre. Toni Morrison and Alice Walker, both the pioneers of African American writings made some revolutionary contributions to literature as, *The Bluest Eye* and *The Colour Purple*, explores the pathos of African American women, traces trauma caused by race and gender biasness and shows the assumed beauty pattern of the West which is not only demotivating but devastating also. Shunning all patriarchal, psychological and social interpretations based on high or low rank, race or colour, both the writers have proved, over time and again, that beauty is no more restricted to white skin and no atrocities can stop a woman to emerge strong and victorious.

The Bluest Eye, inspired by a conversation of Morrison and her friend explores the psychological structure of beauty and its relation to skin color. It explores the hierarchy of white skin, white men and white women over the black ones. Narrative of a small girl Pecola who is looking for love and acceptance eventually fall a victim of racism, psychological devastation and sexual exploitation in the hands of society and her own family. Woven in a narrative of different seasons, the novel traces the dominance of hierarchical beauty standards and its devastating effects on small girl, Pecola. Revolving around African American families of MacTeers and Breedlove who migrated to Lorain – Ohio to earn livelihood the novel traces the journey of both families. Struggling for the acceptance, love, equality and beauty for majority of her life, the protagonist Pecola was more a victim of internalised racism. At tender age of eleven, her parents deserted her and she eventually fall victim in hands of her drunkard father as he raped her. Already longing for blue eyes, a symbol of beauty and acceptance, Pecola after being sexually abused by her father, lost her sanity and eventually gave birth to a child who however died later. Losing her sanity, Pecola believed that God has miraculously blessed her with blue eyes. Similarto Pecola Breedlove, *The Colour Purple's* protagonist, Celie also fell victim in hands of her father as she was raped too. A poor girl maltreated at tender age, Celie became an object of perpetual abuse and later got married to a much older man than her named Mr.____ who tried to control her physically, sexually and mentally. Walker's discrete style of narration through letters to God and the emancipation of her female characters makes, *The Colour Purple* an exemplary work worth appreciation which covers journey of Sister duo – Nettie and Celie through letters and introduces us to some self-loving, confident and bold woman characters like Shug Avery.

III

Racial discrimination, a tendency to prove the domination and hierarchy of one race over the other by means of degrading the other race as inferiors had become an integral part of independent America even after its claim of being just and civilised. Dragging minorities to the corner as subalterns, the victims of racial discrimination either forcefully or by choice eventually tend to accept the so called 'superior' culture and values of the dominant race. Prevalent in America from centuries, the discrimination on basis of race and gender has not only tried to control the African Americans physically but the exploitation was more psychological in nature also. In *The Bluest Eye* and *The Colour Purple*, not only the protagonists Pecola Breedlove and Celie but the full-fledged families have been victims of racial discrimination which itself was a product of racial ideology and prejudice. Pecola Breedlove of *The Bluest eye*, as Morrison portrayed her as an eleven year old girl having obsession with the idea of having blue eyes, a symbol of being beautiful and attractive as she unanimously admired Shirley Temple like all other 'white' girls; "A little black girl who wanted to rise up out of the pit of her blackness and see the world with blue eyes" (Morrison 175). The reason for this obsession has the hidden face of Pecola's dishonoring and abuse by her father and her treatment as 'ugly fur ball' by her mother and society too. The racism here is not societal rather it is an internalised one. Pecola has underestimated and underrated herself by regarding herself ugly while considering the ones with pink skin as beautiful. Her black skin also cornered her from the whole class and the inhumane treatment made her realise the ugliness. She kept watching her own self for hours long; "Long hours she sat looking in the mirror, trying to discover the secret of the ugliness, the ugliness that made her ignored or despised at school, by teachers and classmates alike" (Morrison 45). Mirror and ugliness, here are symbolic to the societal perception and set standards of beauty, which Pecola doesn't match or surpass as per her own understanding. Thus, considering her own self as ugly and unattractive, she reflects how an African American has internalised racism and how it affected his mind and heart. It was not only Pecola, rather her mother Pauline, brother Sammy and her whole family who were made to understand themselves inferior than the white populace; "They lived there because they were poor and black, and they stayed there because they believed they were ugly. Although their poverty was traditional and stultifying, it was not unique. But their ugliness was unique" (Morrison 38). The idea of being ugly, was not only a consequence of their assumption instead they are fed to think and feel inferior and ashamed due to their biologically assigned colour and features. Longing for acceptance and love, Pecola was left by her own parents having 'no place to stay', she was left with MacTeers as her parents' reunion was awaited. Pecola's mother, Pauline was also a victim of racial discrimination which emerged as a result of her own fostering of internalised racism and ambition to settle in the mainstream white culture. After various failed efforts ranging from changing her name to 'Polly' to changing looks and wearing high heels, Mrs. Pauline Breedlove eventually started serving in the house of whites to fulfill her dreams full of grandeur and fancy.

Exemplification of inherited and unconscious racism among white skin people is incident with Young Junior, who was Pecola's schoolmate. He was instructed not to play with black children by his mother Geraldine, who was herself a black woman. Young Junior invited Pecola Breedlove to his house and pranked by throwing a big black cat on her which made her enough scared that she ran around the whole house and eventually got trapped. On witnessing Pecola in her home, Geraldine shouted at her saying pinching racial slurs and called her a nasty bitch. "Get out, she said, her voice quiet. You nasty little black bitch. Get out of my house" (Morrison 92). The racial discrimination was not only individual or internalised but it was also institutional one. Pecola endured the pain, humiliation and inequality at school, home, neighborhood and even market. Once Pecola went to a grocery store where a 52-year old man Mr. Yacobowski cannot acknowledge Pecola's presence as a subject because he simply was not even able to have a glance on her due to her black colour; "How can a fifty-two-year-old white immigrant store-keeper with the taste of potatoes and beer in his mouth, his mind honed on the doe-eyed Virgin Mary, his sensibilities blunted by a permanent awareness of loss, see a little black girl?" (Morrison 48). The psychological devastation of small girl and the mental torture which suffocated Pecola was an upshot of American thinking and values which were inherited and passed on from one generation to another. Based on misogynistic interpretations and sexism what Pecola endured was not a part of any white girl's life. The derogation of Pecola was due to her biologically assigned skin colour, gender and the racial ideology that fostered racism in America. Not only

Pecola but his father Cholly Breedlove also became victim of bullying and exploitation done by two white men. As Cholly was once caught copulating with his girlfriend when they were interrupted by white men who called them with pinching racial slurs and taunted them saying "Get on wid it, nigger, said the flashlight one......I said, get on wid it. An' make it good, nigger, make it good" (Morrison 163).

On a similar tone with *The Bluest Eye*, *The Colour Purple's* protagonist Celie was also a victim of self-hatred and self-consciousness. Celie just like Pecola felt herself inferior to other white people and was a victim of internalised racism. The novel shows an explicit portrayal of sexism, sexual abuse and racial discrimination. Sofia, a black woman also became victim of racism and endured a lot of atrocities, violence and abuse. The inhumane treatment that was given to her made her blind and her ribs got broken. She was made to sleep on a rough cement floor in inhumane conditions. She was accused of sassing the White Mayor's wife, as she was imprisoned her experience was gruesome and painful as she was beaten mercilessly; "They crack her skull, they crack her ribs. They tear her nose loose on one side. They blind her in one eye. She swole from head to foot" (Walker 53). Mayor, his wife and his son were all perpetrators and they abused many blacks either by racial slurs or taunting. The other evidence of racial discrimination and discriminatory ideology can be traced in Nettie's letter to Celie where she describes her train journey to New York. They were made to sit away from the white people, the seating arrangement was discriminatory. The toilets, beds and restaurants for whites and a sit-down section for blacks only is simultaneous to the 'Jim-Crow lane or section'. As Nettie says, "We had to ride in the sit-down section of The train, but Celie, there are beds on trains! And a restaurant! And toilets! The beds come down out of the walls, over the tops of the seats, and are called berths. Only white people can ride in the beds and use the restaurant" (Walker 75). Celie and other women characters witnessed racism throughout their life but her self-emancipation was worth appreciating. The racial discourse made black females realise the fault in their physical beauty and looks which was nothing more than systematic racism, made to make the 'other' race feel inferior.

IV

Abuse, may it be physical, psychological, mental, emotional or in any other form is intolerable and gruesome. The patriarchal view of having binaries of white over black, light over dark and men over women has raged the fire of violence and abuse among many. Many African American women fell victims in hands of either whites or their people of their own race, who in many cases turns out to be their near ones. Men having misogynistic interpretations and prejudice against women tend to misunderstand them as their own property. Both the protagonists, Celie and Pecola endured abuse in their childhood. The astonishment arises from the fact that in cases of both the characters the abuser and perpetrator was their own father. Pecola Breedlove looked for love and affection throughout her life but lastly ended up being raped by Cholly Breedlove. The lusty monster inside Cholly made him enough blind that he hadn't even spared his daughter as he "put his head down and nibbled at the back of her leg. His mouth trembled at the firm sweetness of the flesh. He closed his eyes, letting his fingers dig into her waist" (Morrison 162). Pecola on being impregnated by her father lately gave birth to a child, who was proven dead. All this led to the insanity of Pecola.

In *The Colour Purple*, Celie also endured the sexual abuse by her father Alphonso who told her to keep silent about what has taken place between them. Celie asserted "He start to choke me, saying You better shut up and get used to it. But I don't never git used to it. And now I feels sick every time I be the one to cook" (Walker 8). Celie's exploitation increased after her mother's death and rape became a regular practice for her father. Synonymous to Pecola's condition, Celie was also impregnated twice by her father. She gave birth to two children who were later sold by Alphonso, though Celie thought that they've been killed. Violence and abuse was inflicted on Celie not only by his father, but she was also a victim of domestic violence. She was beaten oftentimes by her husband Mr. ____, as he was extremely controlling and thought Celie to be a breeding machine who is only there for work and enduring his dominating attitude. Celie one requested Mr.___ to take permission for going to Memphis with Shug Avery to which Mr.___ not only reverted negatively but also said, "You bitch, he say. What will people say, you running off to Memphis like you don't have a house to look after?" (Walker 99). Another female who was a victim of rape abuse is Squeak who finds herself identical to Celie as both were being raped forcefully and shares the same pain, the only difference lies between the known and unknown. Celie was abused by her own father whereas Squeak was abused by a white man. The freedom and liberation in life of women seems to be men's property as Celie was first controlled by her father and later her husband tried to be in charge, whereas Pecola was abused and harassed emotionally, physically and mentally, lastly losing her own sanity. All the black women endured and underwent excessive pain in their puzzled life which always seemed controlled by some other dominative power.

V

Oppressions of racism, classism and sexism have been a part of black women's life. In both the novels, the protagonists Pecola Breedlove and Celie along with many other 'black' female characters have been a sufferer of racial discrimination may it be institutional, internalised, or the intra-racial racism. The difference of colour in no sense has been appreciated or celebrated; rather it has always become a matter of debate. African American women have been treated as Subalterns and made feel inferior than the rest of the countrymen living in a phony civilised world. The physical, psychological and sexual abuse has been considered as a part of their lives as they're meant for bearing the atrocities of men and white people. From the childhood, blacks especially the black girl have been treated as less human who have became rape and abuse victims many times in the hands of their owns, "more likely to be exposed to chronic high-impact traumas such as childhood sexual abuse and rape" (Ruglass and Kendall-Tackett 76). The treatment of women as mere livestock is awful in many narratives expressing the black life and experience, psychological devastation and abuse is shown to be a part of black people's life. Though, many black people have emerged as great abolitionist and leaders but the racism has not clearly swiped off till now. As described by Disch, "African American women face a severe disadvantage in society; not only are they part of the subordinate group for gender, they are the subordinate group in regards to race, too" (99).

Works Cited

Abraham, Anjali. 'The Journey of Black Woman from Self Hatred to Self-Love: A Study of Alice Walker's *The Color Purple*." *Smart Moves Journal IJELLH*, vol. 3, no. 5, 17 May 2017, pp. 270–282. July 2015, ijellh.com/OJS/index.php/OJS/article/view/564.

Bharadwaj, Neelam. "*The Bluest Eye*: A Tragedy of Oppression and Internalised Racism." *International Journal on Studies in English Language and Literature* (IJSELL), vol. 4, no. 8, 8 Aug. 2016, pp. 101–104., doi:http://dx.doi.org/10.20431/2347-3134.0408014.

Bring, Maria. *Racism within African American Communities in Toni Morrison's* The Bluest Eye *and* Paradise. New York, 2001.

Disch, Estelle. *Reconstructing Gender: A Multicultural Anthology*. McGraw Hill, 2003.

Frías, María, et al. "An Interview with Toni Morrison, And A Commentary About Her Work." *Atlantis,* vol. 16, no. ½, 1994, pp. 273-83. *JSTOR*, www.jstor.org/stable/41054752. Accessed 24 Jan. 2021.

Morrison, Toni. 'Playing in the Dark: Whiteness and the Literary Imagination." *Racism in America: A Reader*. Harvard UP, 2020, pp. 1-9.

Morrison, Toni. *The Bluest Eye: A Novel.* Vintage International, 2007, The Bluest Eye-Webs, www.google.com/url?sa=t&source=web&rct=j&url=https://memberfiles.freewebs.com/36/26/43092636/documents/Bluest%2520Eye,%2520The%2520-%2520Toni%2520Morrison.pdf&ved=2ahUKEwju1ICokMvuAhXKzDgGHRiGC98QFjAAegQIARAB&usg=AOvVaw2j0rWO4DH1Zxlp8h69vT-O.

Parveen, Dr. Tarana. "Child Abuse in Toni Morrison's *The Bluest Eye*." *International Journal of English Language, Literature and Translation Studies* IJELR, vol. 2, no. 2, 2015, pp. 221–224. www.ijelr.in/2.2.15/221-224%20Dr%20TARANA%20PARVEEN.pdf.

Ruglass, Lesia and Kathleen Kendall-Tackett. *Psychology of Trauma* 101. Springer Publishing Company, 2015.

Simien, Evelyn M. "Black Feminist Theory: Charting a Course for Black Women's Studies in Political Science." *Politics*, vol. 26, no. 2, 2004, pp. 81-93., doi:10.1300/J014v26n02_04.

Walker, Alice. *The Colour Purple.* Open Road Integrated Media, New York, 2011, The Colour Purple-Alice Walker, www.google.com/url?sa=t&source=web&rct=j&url=https://s3.amazonaws.com/scschoolfiles/112/the-color-purple-alice-walker.pdf&ved=2ah

Wikipedia contributors. "George Floyd Protests." Wikipedia, Wikimedia Foundation, 23 Jan. 2021. Accessed 27 Jan. 2021.

Wikipedia contributors. "Misogynoir." Wikipedia, Wikimedia Foundation, 28 Jan. 2021. Accessed 29 Jan. 2021.

Wikipedia contributors. "Racism in the United States." Wikipedia, Wikimedia Foundation, 14 Jan. 2021. Accessed 24 Jan. 2021.

CHAPTER 10

Morrison's *Beloved*: A Postmodern Voice to the Unvoiced Slavery

Radhika

Toni Morrison is one of the prominent authors of contemporary America who deals primarily with the historical plight of Africans living in America. She poignantly portrays how the disadvantage African Americans had to bear the brunt of slavery in America and had to live a life of subjugation and segregation in a society that boasts of being just and equal. Her novels are chronicles of Jim Crow America where 'white is right' and the black Americans were maltreated, exploited and lynched if they would raise voice against slavery and Jim Crow stereotypes being forced on them in the name of superiority of the white race.

African American literature is "a post emancipation phenomenon that gained its coherence as an undertaking in the social world defined by the system of Jim Crow Segregation that ensued after the nations retreat from reconstruction" (Grossberg 1). It articulates the struggle, suffering and pain of the black people that they have gone through in order to liberate themselves from the dominant racial ideology and culture which restricted their social development. It speaks about the oppression, violation and slavery and physical torture faced by the black Americans at the hands of the racist whites. M. H. Abrams rightly opines:

> The complexity and diversity of the African American cultural heritage – both Western and African, oral and written, slave and free, Judeo-Christian and pagan, plantation and urban, integrationist and black nationalist – have effected tensions and fusions that, over the course of time, have produced a highly innovative and distinctive literature. (274)

The escalation of slavery led to an increase in resistance which resulted in the Civil War and, with this, the struggle of the black

Americans came to an end. 19th century is considered to be great revolutionary change that took place in the American literature. Some of the black authors started jotting down their experiences of slavery in one or the other form such as written, oral or slave narratives. These slave narratives not only portrayed the mind and heart of African American but also presented a vivid picture of the lives of the slaves in American society.

In the middle of the 19th century, the black Americans started writing slave narratives which soon became one of the prevailing forms of "Protest literature". This narrative depicted the enslavement and its impact on the lives of the black people. The former slaves, Harriet Jacobs and Frederick Douglas, discussed their personal experiences through slave narratives. After the American civil war, the slavery was abolished and the writers such as W.E. B. Du Bois started highlighting the conditions of the blacks in the U.S through their works. Du Bois in his seminal work, *The Souls of Black Folk* coined the term "Double Consciousness" for the black people. He tinted that black people should be conscious about two visions at a time, that is, how they see themselves in the society and how the society views them. He viewed:

> It is a peculiar sensation, this double-consciousness, this sense of always looking at one's self through the eyes of others, of measuring one's soul by the tape of the world that looks on in amused contempt and pity. One ever feels his two-ness, an American, a Negro; two souls, two thoughts, two unreconciled strivings; two warring ideals in one dark body, whose dogged strength alone keeps it from being torn asunder. The History of the American Negro is the history of this strife – this longing to attain self-conscious manhood, to merge his double self into a better and truer self. He simply wishes to make it possible for a man to be both a Negro and an American, without being cursed and spit his face. (2-3)

Frederic Douglas also agreed to the concept of Du Bois and noted that literacy is "the pathway from slavery to freedom" (*Reading Black, Reading Feminist* 49).

In the early 1920's, Harlem Renaissance started which came out to be the cultural expression for the African Americans. It was a period of "creativity in literature, music, dance, painting and sculptures by African Americans" (Abrams 157). Writers such as Langston Hughes, Zora Neale Hurston, Claude McKay etc. gave new identity to the African Americans. The members of this movement produced various art forms that depicted the realistic picture of being black in the white society. Langston Hughes called this movement an "expression of our individual dark-skinned selves" (*The Negro Artist and the Racial Mountain* 5).

The works that were transmitted from Harlem illustrated the actual life, culture and identities of the African Americans. Harlem Renaissance not only introduced the African American culture but also inculcated the willpower and the pride of the blacks, their consciousness and their dedication to the political activism. With the emergence of this "New Negro Movement" it was for the first time when white society became conscious about the conditions of the blacks. Richard Wright's *Native Son* and Ralph Ellison's *Invisible Man* gave recognition to the blacks and their identities were seen with a new dimension.

African American literature focused on the brutality and poverty that critically impacted the lives of the blacks, especially, the black women. Harriet Jacobs through her autobiography *Incidents in the Life of a Slave Girl* (1861) foregrounded that slavery was dreadful for women. African American women were always the subject to wrongs and sufferings. In the mid-20th century, the black women writers took hold over portraying their characters, especially, the female characters with sincerity and imagination. The works of the writers were the representation of an open revolt against the doctrines that put black women into the category of suppressed class. Through their writings, they gave a new vision to the importance of mothering, sexuality and spirituality. The black women writing gave a new direction and development of the African American literature. Hortense Spillers, a feminist critic, rightly said, "The community of black women writing in the United States now (1970) can be regarded as a vivid new fact of national life" (Gates 34).

Most of the black women writers talked about racism, slavery, oppression and equality. They strive to give voice to the silenced or 'damaged' women merely because of their valour of being black women. Michele Wallace distinctly stated that "being at the bottom, they would have to do what no one else has done-fight the world" (20).

The black women writers not only voice the sufferings of black men but also highlighted the circumstances that were being faced by black women. Through their works they try to give an optimistic definition of 'Self' and 'Blackness'. According to Stacey and Laura:

> Black women, through their fictions imagine and create a space for both the subversion of oppressive sociopolitical structures and the possibility for libratory self-determination. Black women's radical subjectivity shatters the boundaries of geopolitical spaces that traditionally have been defined through citizenship and creates alternatives social imaginaries that represent a space where home and belongingness may be attained and self-determination realised. (Gillis 529)

Writers like Alice Walker, Toni Morrison, Maya Angelou and others portrayed the true picture of black women that were earlier neglected by white writers and black male writers. Their writings brought a new dimension to the "suppressed and silenced", which is, amalgamation of black and woman. Gates in his book *Reading Black, Reading Feminist*, expressed:

> If there is a single distinguishing feature of the literature of Black women – and this accounts for their lack of recognition – it is this: their literature is about Black women; it takes the trouble to record the thoughts, words, feelings and deeds of black women, experiences that make the realities of being black in America look very different from what men have written ... women talk to other women in this tradition, and their relationships with other women – mothers, sisters, grandmothers, friends, lovers – are vital to their growth and well-being. (Gates 35)

Toni Morrison, one of the flourishing African American women writers, has created her female characters in such a way that they go against all the conventional norms of womanhood. Her main concern is that how the damaged psyche of an individual can affect human behaviour. Morrison makes black women her centre of attraction and tries to liberate them from silence and absence by giving them voice. The protagonists of her novels, such as *The Bluest Eye, Sula* and *Beloved* seek to create their own identity by raising them above their oppressed state. The novels show the psychological impact on the characters while living in a culture where their own self is questioned by the domination of slavery.

Morrison constructs her Pulitzer Prize winning novel *Beloved* (1987) as a postmodern voice that gives the impression of slavery and its impact on the conscious and subconscious minds. It is a historical novel which demonstrates the hard reality of slavery that was being faced by both men and women. She tries to combine the past slavery with present freedom. In fact, Peterson asserts:

> Morrison has spent her career questioning the premises of history and historical writing, particularly as they pertain to African Americans and the representation of African American history. The goal of her fiction... has been not just to recover details of African American history, but to choose which details are useful for "the village" or the community in the struggle to create a past that can enable African Americans to have in the words of Beloved, a "livable life" in the present and future. (202)

Beloved is a story that was stimulated by an actual incident of an African American slave, Margaret Garnar. She escaped from slavery and with a fear of being caught by her master, she chose to kill her children instead of opting forced slavery for them. Morrison elucidates it, "a women loved something other than herself so much. She had placed all of the values of her life in something outside herself. That the woman who killed her children loved her children so much; they were the best part of her and she would not see them sullied" (*Playing in the Dark* 584).

The protagonist of the novel, Sethe, also kills her daughter in order to save her from the terrible experiences of slavery. Throughout the novel, she is haunted by the brutal and cruel actions done on her by her slave master. Being a slave, she was always harassed by her master. She tries to move on in her life but her past experiences of slavery pulled her back to those vicious molestations. Sethe tries her best to escape from those tormented memories of slavery but instead of moving away from those memories she is entrapped in them.

Toni Morrison not only discusses the incident of Sethe's rape by her master while her husband was forced to watch that. Instead she also talks about the dishonor caused to Sethe when two of her master's nephews sucked her milk from her breast. Morrison quoted, "their bodies not supposed to be like that, but they have to have as many children as they can to please whoever owned them" (*Beloved* 5).

The plot of the novel revolves around the heartache of the lost mothers, Beloved's pain for Sethe; Sethe's mourning for Baby Suggs; Sethe's hammering her own mother. Sethe remembers her mother in piercing fragments, "a hat in the rice field, a scar under the breast" (Beloved 61). Sethe was suckled by the plantation nurse as her mother was sent to the fields, "the little white babies got it first and I got what was left. Or none. There was no nursing milk to call my own. I know what it is to be without the milk that belongs to you…" (Beloved 200). This manifold bereavement for mothers carves the tragic experience of African American children and women.

The unbearable, severe and painful incidents haunt Sethe throughout her life. She was not able to come out of these terrible experiences. She promised herself that irrespective of any situation she would always be available for her children and will provide her milk to them. For Sethe, milk was not only a necessity for her children but it was her love for them which she never got from her mother. The memory of Sethe's mother not only depict the pain of her alone but is the symbol of the discomfort felt by all the African slave mothers. These slaves always struggled for their babies and above them for their own identities. Sethe never wanted her children to feel the same void that she felt in her life because of the absence of her mother. She considered the incident of killing her children as their own fate.

But the ghost which is regarded as the incarnation of Sethe's dead daughter, Beloved, haunts her, reminds her of the guilt of murdering and points out the inhuman side of slavery. The act of homicide was done in context of Sethe's horrible past experiences as a slave and how it impacted her psyche. Her psyche was wounded so badly that she was detached from the outside world. Every time she sees the ghost of Beloved, she is forced to recall her slave experiences. It is because Beloved is not only considered as the ghost of a dead daughter but also the phantom of slavery that depicts the cruelty, sadistic and harsh reality of subjugation.

Denver is also able to see the ghost of Beloved, "a white dress knelt down next to her mother and had its sleeve around her mother's waist" (*Beloved* 29). She embraces the return of her sister. She grew up as an only child and is happy with the company of Beloved. There are a number of significant ways in which Denver is connected to Beloved, among them, the main is that they both are born to the same mother. The most thoughtful detail that connects both the sisters is their mother's milk. After Beloved's violent death Denver "took her mother's milk right along with the blood of her sister" (*Beloved* 152).

It is Beloved who is wounded and deprived. She is the one who indicates the worst act of brutality caused because of the fear of slavery and it is an outcome of not only the physical death of an individual but also the psychological death. When Sethe feels that her worthiness is being destroyed by her slave master, she murders her own daughter with an aim of protecting her from inhuman experiences and mainly from the psychological death which she herself is facing in the life. Sethe makes it clear that "if I hadn't killed her she would have died and this is something I could not bear to happen to her" (200). The intellectual and emotional scars of slavery are so deep that even if people are free from the conditions and experiences of slavery, their thoughts would not let them free themselves from those horrors. Sethe points out that, "freeing yourself was one thing; claiming ownership of that freed self was another" (95).

With the appearance of Beloved, the change emerges in the psyche of other characters – Paul D, Denver and Sethe. They understand that it is menacing to hang on to the past and one needs to look forward for a brighter future. They realised that they need to learn from their experiences and try to shape their future without being cursed by their past feelings. Seethe soon overcomes the guilt of killing her daughter and starts ignoring the ghost of beloved.

> They forgot her like a bad dream. After they made up their tales, shaped and decorated them, those that saw her that day on the porch quickly and deliberately forgot her. It took longer for those who had spoken to her, to forget, until they realised they couldn't remember or repeat a single thing she said, and began to believe that, other than what they themselves were thinking she hadn't said anything at all. So, in the end, they forgot her too. (274)

Beloved not only talks about the life and struggle of Sethe alone but projects the collective consciousness of all the suppressed voices. It narrates the miserable story of the sufferings of the black people and the necessity to overcome those pains. Toni Morrison gives her characters the power to speak through her own voice. In the novel, she depicts the vivid time of slavery and also represented the depressed and dehumanised identities of African Americans. Morrison's women are linked together in a chain of pain and grief. Sethe's mother desires her daughter to recognise her body by the scar 185 under her breast; Sethe has "chokecherry tree" mark on her back which is the scar of brutal beating; Sethe's revived daughter bears a mark of her mother's handsaw on her neck. Simone de Beauvoir has rightly said, "the women of today are in a fair way to dethrone the myth of femininity; they are beginning to affirm their independence in concrete ways; but they do not easily succeed in living completely the life of human being" (31).

African Americans had been the victims of brutality, oppression, subjugation and cruelty throughout their slavery. They had faced extreme molestations such as rape, genocides, slaughtering and lynching. Due to these experiences they were the sufferers of trauma, hopelessness and fretfulness. Slavery was a curse for them which left scars on their psyche and which even offended their inner peace. For them freedom was another kind of trauma because they were free from slavery but not from the experiences they faced. Keeping these experiences alive and connecting the present freedom with the past slavery, African American writers have constructed a rich and zestful literary form that has become one of the dominant and distinctive feature of African American literature and its culture. Their works carry critical and silenced memories of the slave system. They give voice to the oppressed and subjugated. These writings not only represents the experiences but also depicts the inner psyche of all those who were the victims of slavery and how their wounds harmed them physically and mentally. These sufferings traveled from generation to generation and the black writers try to bring out the inner self of the sufferers by becoming their mouthpiece.

Work Cited

Abrams, M.H. and Geoffrey Galt Harpham. *A Glossary of Literary Terms.* Cengage Learning India Private Limited, 2013.

Beauvoir, Simone de. *The Second Sex.* Translated and edited by H.M. Parshley. Pan Books, 1988.

Du Bois, W.E.B. *The Souls of Black Folk.* Penguin, 1903.

Fanon, Frantz. *Black Skin, White Masks.* Pluton Press, 1986.

Gates, Henry Louis Jr., editor. *Reading Black, Reading Feminist.* Meridian, 1990.

Gillis, Stacey, et. al., editors. *Third Wave Feminisim: A Critical Exploration.* Palgrave Macmillan, 2007.

Grossberg, Larry and Janice Radway, editors. *Cultural Studies: Toni Morrison and Curriculum.* Special edition, edited by Warren Crichton and Cameron McCarthy, Routledge, vol. 9, no. 2, 1995.

Hughes, Langston. *The Collected Works of Langston Hughes.* U of Missouri P, 1942.

Morrison, Toni. *Beloved.* Picador, 1987.

---. *Playing in the Dark: Whiteness and the Literary Imagination.* Vintage Books, 1992.

Peterson, Nancy J. *Toni Morrison: Critical and Theoretical Approches.* John Hopkins UP, 1997.

CHAPTER 11

Postmodernism in the Writings of Toni Morrison

Upanisha S.

Postmodernism, a phenomenon that began in the mid and late twentieth century involving the fields of art, architecture, and literature attempts skepticality towards the grand narratives of modernity, applying Derrida's concept of deconstruction to it. Morrison's works in a like vein deconstruct the psyche of the African American to reveal the trauma inflicted upon him through the ages, as a result of the prolonged effect of slavery, followed by other calamities like racism, and the withholding of civil liberties.

Morrison's language in itself subscribes to the standards prescribed by Henry Louis Gates, Jr. of the signifying, a beautiful melange of metaphor, irony, metalepsis, metaphor, litotes, and synecdoche, which is both epigrammatic of the style of postmodernism, as well as that of African American literature. Morrison also employs stream of consciousness technique in order to retain the flow of thoughts and memories of various characters, and augment the poignancy of their circumstances. The language of Morrison also flows with the cadences of poetry, and plain conversations resonate with the curtsies and shimmies of dance:

> Their conversation is like a gently wicked dance; sound meets sound, curtsies, shimmies, and retires. Another sound enters but is upstaged by still another: the two circle each other and stop. Sometimes their words move in lofty spirals; other times they take strident leaps, and all of it punctuated with warm pulsed laughter – like the throb of a heart made of jelly. The edge, the curl, the thrust of their emotions is always clear to Frieda and me. We do not, cannot know the meaning of all their words, for we are nine and ten years old. So, we watch their faces, their hands, their feet and listen for truth in timber. (*The Bluest Eye* 9-10)

Even though Morrison is making an effort to bring out the plight of the African American community, her narrative abounds with positivity, such as Paul D's description of the flowers that guided him to the north, and Claudia's description of a wonderful Christmas at her grandparents' house.

> 'I want to sit on the low stool in Big Mama's kitchen with my lap full of lilacs and listen to Big Papa play his violin for me alone.' The lowness of the stool made for my body, the security and warmth of Big Mama's kitchen, the smell of the lilacs, the sound of the music, and, since it would be good to have all of my senses engaged, the taste of a peach, perhaps, afterward. (The *Bluest Eye* 15).

Beloved begins with a perfect example of the use of the stream of consciousness technique with Sethe's introduction oscillating from 124, Bluestone Road to Sweet Home. There is also a background of musicality to Morrison's novels – the blues aesthetic in *The Bluest Eye*, and the Jazz aesthetic in *Jazz*. Even individual scenes are often represented musically.

> It started that way: laughing children, dancing men, crying women and then it got mixed up. Women stopped crying and danced; men sat down and cried; children danced, women laughed, children cried until, exhausted and riven, all and each lay about the Clearing damp and gasping for breath. In the silence that followed, Baby Suggs holy, offered up to them her great big heart. (*Beloved* 103)

Aesthetics apart, Morrison also caters to the yardstick of a political narrative which is yet another hallmark of postmodernism. Morrison desires her work to be a memorial to the more than sixty million people who bore the brunt of slavery, and its aftermath, especially the women, who bore the dual anguish of both patriarchy, as well as racism. The men are also taken along on a journey of equality that epitomises womanism.

In the telling of the tale of trauma, Morrison employs the use of folklore, common to the African American culture. The primer of *The Bluest Eye* itself begins with the Dick and Jane story which elevates into a refrain as the story progresses. Baby Suggs' sermons in the Clearing also resemble a village gathering, and when the women gather to exorcise the ghost of Beloved, it reflects the hoodoo tradition, also close to the African American community. Readers can even encounter the case of a man flying in *Song of Solomon*.

Thus the plethora of complex tropes used by Morrison helps to contextualise the racist trauma experienced by Morrison's characters. In this way Morrison panders to the norm of pluralism which is the cornerstone of postmodernism. Morrison's novels also end on a note of ambiguity which denotes skepticism, which is the hallmark of postmodernism.

Postmodernism is often criticised for obscurity and skepticism. Morrison however uses this obscurity and skepticism to her advantage, leading to beautifully ambiguous endings, which offer space for the reader to interpret his or her own conclusions, and thus allowing these readers to decide whether the stories should or should not be passed on.

Morrison's skepticism towards a better life for her community is also displayed in several novels like *Sula*, in which the African American community is shown struggling to hold down stable jobs in the middle of such events as the St. Louis riots, depicted in *Jazz*. Morrison has even expressed skepticism about humanism in several televised interviews. Though Morrison has attempted to portray the situation of her people through the ages, the struggle still continues.

Another prominent quality of postmodernist writing is that of self-reflexivity, which is produced aplenty by Morrison in her works. Morrison has professed in many interviews that she has always striven to produce works of literature that she would herself have enjoyed reading. To this end *The Bluest Eye* was written. Morrison's love of motherhood has also made her centre many of her novels around mother figures like Mrs. MacTeer, Pauline Breedlove, Aunt Jimmy, Eva Peace, Helene Sabat, Sethe, Alicia Manfred, and Connie, to name just a few.

The story of *Beloved* is also based on Morrison's reading of the story of Margaret Garner, a fugitive slave who attempted to murder her children, while *Jazz* is Morrison's interpretation of a picture taken by James Van Der Zee of a young lady who had been shot dead by a lover. *Jazz* also has the backdrop of the St. Louis riots, perhaps brought on by Morrison's father's narration of a lynching that he had witnessed. Morrison also voices her protest towards normative religious beliefs by Reverend Misner's visualisation of a Black Jesus Christ in *Paradise*.

As regards the aspect of metanarratives as well, Morrison brings in a unique brand of storytelling, which involves aspects of traditional African American features of storytelling which were a staple at Morrison's own dinner table – the appearance of ghosts, the laying on of the hands, the alternative remedies offered by M'Dear, and also little things like the playing of the banjos, the cakewalk, and the Black Bottom.

Morrison also uses multiple voices in her narrative technique, bringing in a pluralistic perspective to her stories. Morrison goes so far as to make the city of New York appear as the narrator in *Jazz*, while in *Beloved* the story is narrated from the varying perspectives of Sethe, Paul D, and sometimes even Stamp Paid.

While numerous analysts of the works of Toni Morrison allude to the influence that the classics have had on her writings, a lot of intertextuality can also be found within the works of Toni Morrison. The novels seem to be a composite whole, each story being intertwined with the next. Sula is the version of beauty that Pecola had always hoped for, and Beloved becomes the mother's little darling that Sula wished to be, transforming into Wild, following her exorcism, and culminating in the women of the Convent.

Morrison also adds to the pluralism by bringing in the mindset of several generations, from former slaves, to emancipated slaves, to people settling up exclusivist townships, to people looking for new opportunities in burgeoning cities. The lived experience of everyone, from little children, to the aged is offered.

Toni Morrison also displays diversity in postmodern thought, bringing in her own unique aspects of dream reality, and the art of stepping in, into the traditional gamut of hoodoo culture. This is beautifully juxtaposed with the variation in the blues and jazz aesthetic brought in by Morrison.

> Gradually they lost the days.
>
> In the beginning the most important thing was the template. First they had to scrub the cellar floor until its stones were as clean as rocks on a shore. Then they ringed the place with candles. Consolafa told each to undress and lie down. In flattering light under Consolata's soft vision they did as they were told. How should we lie? However you feel. They tried arms at the sides, outstretched above the head, crossed over breasts or stomach. Seneca lay on her stomach at first, then changed to her back, hands clasping her shoulders. Pallas lay on her side, knees drawn up. Gigi flung her legs and arms apart, while Mavis struck a floaters pose, arms angeled, knees pointing in. When each found the position she could tolerate on the cold, uncompromising floor, Consolata walked around her and painted the body's silhouette. Once the outlines were complete, each was instructed to remain there. Unspeaking. Naked in candlelight. (*Paradise* 262-263)
>
> 'Step in. Just step on in. Help him, girl!'
>
> Consolata looked at the body and without hesitation removed her glasses and focused on the trickles of red discoloring his hair. She stepped in. Saw the stretch of road he had dreamed through, felt the flip of the truck, the

headache, the chest pressure, the unwillingness to breathe. As from a distance she heard Easter and July kicking the truck and moaning. Inside the boy she saw a pinpoint of light receding. Pulling up energy that felt like fear, she stared at it until it widened. Then more, more, so air could come seeping, at first, then rushing rushing in. Although it hurt like the devil to look at it, she concentrated as though the lungs in need were her own. (*Paradise* 245)

This is comparable to:

...A city like this one makes me dream tall and feel in on things. Help. It's the bright steel rocking above the shade below that does it. When I look over strips of green grass lining the river, at church steeples and into the cream-and-copper halls of apartment buildings, I'm strong. Alone, yes, but top-notch and indestructible – like the City in 1926 when all the wars are over and there will never be another one. The people down there in the shadow are happy about that. At last, at last everything's ahead. The smart ones say so and people listening to them and reading what they write down agree: Here comes the new. Look out. There goes the sad stuff. The bad stuff. The things-nobody-could-help stuff. The way everybody was then and there. Forget that. History is over, you all, and everything's ahead at last. (*Jazz* 7)

'When I first seed Cholly, I want you to know it was like all the bits of color from that time down home when all us children went berry picking after a funeral and I put some in the pocket of my Sunday dress, and they mashed up and stained my hips. My whole dress was messed with purple, and it never did wash out. Not the dress nor me. I could feel that purple deep inside me. And that lemonade Mama used to make when Pap came in out the fields. It be cool and yellowish, with seeds floating near the bottom. And that streak of green them june bugs made on the trees the night we left from down home. All of them colors was in me. Just sitting there. So when Cholly come up and tickled my foot, it was like them berries, that lemonade, them streaks of green the June bugs made, all come together. Cholly was thin then, with real light eyes. He used to whistle, and when I heard him, shivers come on my skin'. (The Bluest Eye 90)

Morrison style of writing yields itself very easily to an inherent musicality, which adds weight to her writing qualifying as metanarrative.

...on quiet days people in valley houses could hear singing sometimes, banjos sometimes, and, if a valley man happened to have business up in those hills – collecting rent or insurance payments – he might see a dark woman in a flowered dress doing a bit of cakewalk, a bit of black bottom, a bit of 'messing around' to the lively notes of a mouth organ. Her bare feet would raise the saffron dust that floated down on the coveralls and bunion-split shoes of the man breathing music in and out of his harmonica. The black people watching her would laugh and rub their knees, and it would be easy for the valley man to hear the laughter and not notice the adult pain that rested somewhere under the eyelids, somewhere under their head rags and soft felt hats, somewhere in the palm of the hand, somewhere behind the frayed lapels, somewhere in the sinew's curve. (*Sula* 4)

> ...Their voices blended into a threnody of nostalgia about pain. Rising and falling, complex in harmony, uncertain in pitch, but constant in the recitative of pain. (*The Bluest Eye* 107)
>
> After situating herself on a huge flat-sided rock, Baby Suggs bowed her head and prayed silently. The company watched her from the trees. They knew she was ready when she put her stick down. Then she shouted, 'Let the children come!' and they ran from the trees toward her.
>
> 'Let your mothers hear you laugh,' she told them, and the woods rang. The adults looked on and could not help smiling.
>
> Then 'Let the grown men come, 'she shouted. They stepped out one by one from among the ringing trees.
>
> 'Let your wives and your children see you dance,' she told them, and ground life shuddered under their feet.
>
> Finally she called the women to her. 'Cry,' she told them. 'For the living and the dead. Just cry. And without covering their eyes the women let loose.
>
> It started that way: laughing children, dancing men, crying women and then it got mixed up. Women stopped crying and danced; men sat down and cried; children danced, women laughed, children cried until, exhausted and riven, all and each lay about the Clearing damp and gasping for breath. In the silence that followed, Baby Suggs, holy, offered up to them her great big heart.
>
> (*Beloved* 102-103)

In this way Morrison weaves a complex narrative, not only attempting to counter standards of race and gender, but also drawing the focus on nuanced aspects like the woman's freedom to express her sensuality through characters like China, Poland, Miss. Marie, Sula, Eva, Hannah, and even Dorcas. Thus, in the plethora of diversity that Morrison affords, she can truly be read as a postmodernist writer.

Works Cited

Gilroy, Paul. *The Black Atlantic: Modernity and Double Consciousness.* Versco 1993.

Morrison, Toni. *Beloved.* Vintage, 2005.

---. *Jazz.* Vintage, 2016.

---. *Paradise.* Vintage, 1999.

---. *Sula.* Vintage, 2005.

---. *The Bluest Eye.* Vintage, 1999.

Peterson, Dale E. *Up from Bondage: The Literatures of Russian and African American Soul.* Duke UP, 2000.

Spargo, Clifton R. et al, editors. *After Representation: The Holocaust, Literature, and Culture.* Rutgers UP, 2000.

CHAPTER 12

Leslie Marmom Silko's *Ceremony* and N. Scott Momaday's *House Made for Dawn*: Reflection of Postmodern American Essence

Vijaykumar Ganpatrao Pawar

> How could people like these, without words to put to their emotions and passions, manage? They could, at best, only suffer dumbly. Their pains and humiliations would work themselves out in their characters alone: like evil spirits possessing a body, so that the body itself might appear innocent of what it did. (Naipaul 48)

The similarity between Leslie Marmon Silko and N. Scott Momaday is their natural ability to delineate the socio-psychological condition of the contemporary period which is possibly best reflected in their characters than their other contemporaries. Their works prominently show psychologically deformed characters due to socio-cultural uncertainty and devastating consequences of two world wars. The novels *Ceremony* and *House Made of Dawn* place its protagonists Tayo and Abel respectively in similar kind of uncertain and unpredictable environment where they go through tremendous hardships, socio-psychological trauma and contrasting situations at the backdrop of moral, social and economical degradation due to the destructions caused by the World War II. The destruction, negativity and hopeless conditions of the age weakened able and strong people and made them helpless and vulnerable. The protagonists Abel and Tayo show the same inability to choose one from their roots and ultimately meet their doom. Once war heroes, brave and courageous, Abel and Tayo are represent meek and scared on account of obsessed war memories, destruction, root, culture and ethnicity. Their goal in the post-world war age is to re-orient their lives and live peacefully. They are portrayed as the war-victims by both the writers. Their seemingly recklessness and audacity stand disillusioned and dismayed at the end of the day. Their disillusionment is realistically pictured by the writers in the form of the shifting of their dream from America to India and vice-versa, which possibly has no destination of its own.

Leslie Marmon Silk's begins his novel *Ceremony* by introducing three poems that have significant value in the Pueblo tradition. The first poem in the series of three is *Ts' its'tsi'nako* that means *Thought Woman* connects all important events in the novel and it is assumed that the story is narrated by the woman. The second poem entitled *Ceremony* that narrates the stories in which people in American societies are fighting with diseases, problems and deaths but are committed strong against all evils. The stories that are narrated in *Ceremony* co-relate to Pueblo culture and the Native American Tradition.

The novel *Ceremony* revolves around its protagonist Tayo, a young Native American protagonist, who has recently returned to his homeland in America after experiencing the horrors and destructions of World War II. During the war, he was captivated by the Japanese army. The devastating consequences the World War and experiences of captivity had almost converted him into a pessimistic that hates life and discards all fortunes and pleasures the world offers to him. Being the person of mixed breed, his experiences within and outside the country, were very acute and painful. The story shows him to be a knight surrounded by mere dead bodies where he tries to sooth himself by thinking of deer and other childhood attractions. It is more or less exposuse and exploration of the aftermaths of war. It explicitly explains the impact of war on its protagonist Tayo's socio-cultural conscience. The writer shows that the dreams of Tayo are a part and parcel of his hybrid cultures; that is pueblo culture. The pueblo culture has been observed by all of Tayo's ancestors therefore it is mandatory for him too.

The land where Tayo lives is shown facing drought since last four years and he feels that it is because he had prayed God to stop rain during war time. His belief that God listens to him is his assumption, for he thinks that due to his blaming of rain, he is the real cause of the drought the land is facing for long four years. The war memories are too painful for him as he lost his dear brother Rakesh in the war. Moreover, belonging to minor community also has had horrible experiences from the fellow countrymen. Tayo experiences a number of darker aspects of war like: bloodshed, racial dominance, dislocation, disintegration of psychology and ultimately a sense of nihilism. The thing he learnt from all of his experience is return to his own roots that is; 're-*orientation*' and '*a return*' to his original ethnicity. Thus *Ceremony* reveals bitter and suffocative experiences of Indian based communities living in America, having been fought and lost lives for the dear land and ultimately the nation, the minor and different cultured people remain neglected and often exploited in the country.

Quite similar is the story and destiny of Abel, the protagonist of *House Made of Dawn*, to Tayo of *Ceremony*. Unlike Tayo, Abel also belongs to socio-culturally hybrid community which is quite unique and different from the dominant cultures in America with their heterogeneous feelings, gestures and expressions. The experiences of Abel are very similar to that of Tayo as he also faces same kind of cultural diversity, and strange and vehement response from the dominant culture forces him to withdraw himself from the society. *House Made of Dawn* opens on the same lines of *Ceremony* as it starts with the return of its protagonist Abel to his native land. After devastating and destructive nightmares of war, it was like dream coming true returning to the native land. On his return, he gets completely mesmerised with the childhood memories of his beloved grandfather and the traditions and rituals of Pueblo culture. The death of his grandfather left him completely collapsed physically and psychologically. Since this point, Abel is shown exhibiting a sense of loss and emptiness of services: disillusioned estranged and broken for entire life.

The novel starts with Abel's entry to which the writer describes as the 'hardest' and 'breathless' to indicate Abel's eagerness and enthusiasm to meet and embrace his motherland. He was away from his native place for longer time and when it comes to meet the beloved land, he can't control his emotions and movements. His running fast and breathless is symbolically represented by the writer as the '*Radical Act of Escape*' from what his life offers as the return to his geographical dislocation. It also symbolically represents his '*Denial to Socio-Cultural Hybridisation*' and signifies his act of '*A Complete Withdrawal*' from the society itself. He is shown half naked and his hands and shoulders stained with burnt wood ashes, as if he is returning from the bloody war.

We observe that both the protagonists, Tayo and Abel, show their denial in the very beginning and in the end. Both the protagonists are shown brooding for self-identity, embracing their native land and their cultural roots. But unfortunately they meet with frustration and psychological disintegration only. Abel quite brilliantly shows his cultural disintegration and emptiness of life and identifies hybrid culture and plural ethnicity to be the real causes:

> There was only the dark infinity in which nothing was. And something happened. At the distance of a star something happened, and everything began. The word did not come into being, but it was. It did not break upon the silence, but it was older than the silence and the silence was made of it. (Momaday 97)

Tayo's suffering in *Ceremony* highlights the problems of cultural identity and puts the character on the constant and continues search of self-identity. Basically, the novel exposes white man's cultural discrimination towards Native American people. Tayo's mother was Native American woman while his biological father was white American. His father never meets him on account of his half-breed birth. All of his life Tayo receives disregard, neglect and humiliation. His father being a white man, Tayo happens to go close to his white relatives and very closely he experiences discrimination and indifferent attitude of white men towards native people. Thus the white world of America was very near to him as well as very far, almost unattainable due to secondary and unequal treatment given to him by his white relatives.

Tayo and Abel show same kind of attraction and preferences to the native cultures like: Laguna, Pueblo, and New Mexico. White men's discriminatory attitude is reflected in the character of Tayo's father who immediately abandons his family soon after his birth. His mother Laura comes from that community where giving birth to a child was always undesirable. Women were considered as a pleasurable thing and not more than that:

> He was four years old the night his mother left him there. He didn't remember much: only that she had come after dark and wrapped him in a man's coat – it smelled like a man – and that there were men in the car with them [...], and he had dozed and listened, half dreaming their laughter and the sound of a cork squeaking in and out of the bottle. (Silko 41)

His single mother was unable to take care of Tayo therefore she leaves him in the custody of her only relative. But Tayo was the unwelcome guest for the auntie who ill-treats him on account of his mother's misdeed that tarnished family reputation. Auntie's son Rocky was close and considerate to Tayo. Both of them join Army and participate in World War Second. However, Rocky gets killed in the war and Tayo, unfortunately survived with lot of destructive and dark memories to live with...

Both Tayo and Abel respond to the uneven and humiliating treatment of the white world with positivity and stubbornness hoping for the change in the behaviour of the predators. Their utmost effort in facing all the problems they faced in white people's country like sense of neglect and unwillingness to accept them as individuals, hostility, cruelty, dislocation and their past memories are either neglected or sought a stance of withdrawal from life itself. Both the novels *House Made of Dawn* and *Ceremony* cover the similar range of thematic concerns, with greater emphasis on the exploration the Pueblo culture and traditions. Silko and Mommaday explicitly exhibit the confrontation faced by colored people at the hands of native white people; it is the confrontation between the two dominant cultures of America: Pueblo and White American culture. The writers intentionally portray their protagonists showing love and affinity towards their birth culture. They are adamant for their roots and root lands. They are shown to be buried under the heavy load of past memories which they cannot at any cost throw away. Their soul is burdened with the sad and painful past memories of killings, massacres and massive war weapons. They experience indomitable dominance of white culture in all fields of life.

In the given background of society where socio-economic crisis and cultural and racial atrocities were rampant, the psychological disintegration was must which has been portrayed by Silko and Momday through their characters. The novels selected here particularly represent the contemporary society and its mentality. The writers exhibit the cross-cultural exchange that had been noticed generally among the people of the age. They, arguably show that the people in the era were looking for escape from mutual existence of diverse cultures, races, ethnicities, etc. Their representation of life and manners incorporating a sense of loss, disappointment, humiliation and withdrawal from almost everything in life, is what is characterised in the contemporary period. Cultural conflict leads them for search of identity which ultimately is inaccessible or unattainable.

Works Cited

Momaday, N. Scott. *House Made of Dawn.* Harper and Row, 1968.

Naipaul, V.S. *The Enigma of Arrival: A Novel in Five Sections.* Viking Press, 1987.

Silko, Leslie Marmon. *Ceremony.* A Penguin Book, 1977.

CHAPTER 13

Postmodern Canons and American Literature

Anum Mirza

Introduction

Frederic Jameson's postmodern aesthetics excited great interest among the cultural critics and reviewers and the philosophers of American society. Hegel was a prominent German thinker and philosopher; a scholar of Tubingen and explored the philosophical ideas of Immanuel Kant and Fichte and Russell. Hegel's philosophy is the culmination of the movement of German philosophy. Hegel wrote his seminal book the *Phenomenology of Spirit* (1807). Hegel came under the influence of French Rationalism, British empiricism and the transcendental philosophy of Immanuel Kant. The philosophical ideas of the Romantics also influenced Hegel. He dedicated his whole life to explore the mystery of truth and envisages a philosophical theory which incorporates all knowledge developing a totalising philosophy comprehending reality. The main focus of Hegel is to integrate all the ideas found in art, religion and literature. Jameson initiated the debate on Marxist post-structuralism by publishing his book *Marxism and Form* which generated huge interest in American readers. *Postmodernism* or *The Cultural Logic of Late Capitalism* (1990) of Frederic Jameson's is regarded as the bible of postmodernism. His more recent works include *Valences of the Dialectics* (2009), *The Antinomies of Realism* (2013) and *The Ancients and the Postmoderns* (2015). Jameson in his *Postmodernism* used the term "late modernism". The modern writers were impacted by the events of Depression, Stalinism, Jewish Holocaust and new concepts of Socialism. Authors of Post-modernism are not much concerned with social realism but use the techniques of Dadaism and Surrealism. Malcolm Bradbury avers thus:

> After 1945 the novel showed every sign of reasserting its realistic potential, its moral and social concern, its sense of life as progress. The lessons of the great moderns...had been taken, but they were assimilated back into a spirit relative realism, and technical and epistemological questions were not strongly pressed. (10)

Characteristics of Postmodern: Black Humor in the Fiction of John Updike

Jameson in his book *Postmodernism* or *The Cultural Logic of Late Capitalism* (1990) discussed in detail the changing trends of contemporary American society and discarded modern techniques. He propounded new styles and literary devices in his book and highlighted the characteristics of postmodernism. Jameson rejects techniques employed by the modern writers and evolving his own perception of reality. The postmodern writers such as John Updike, Vladimir Nabokov, Flannery O'Conner, Bernard Malamud and John Cheever used the postmodern techniques in their fiction. The prose of John Updike has "the sharpness of a surgeon's scalpel, the precision of a fine watch and focuses on the commonplace like the eye of an X-ray machine". The eye of John Updike is very sharp and he sees with the eye of a bird. John Updike doesn't depend on the reality of events of the past like Hemingway but he creates a new world as his vision is apocalyptic. The postmodern novelists created a galaxy of characters mostly belonging to the middle class America confronting the uncertainties and absurdities of life involved in a world of despair. Their protagonists are absurd struggling in a world of science and technology and trapped in a godless universe. For example, John Updike in his novel *Rabbit Run* Harry Angstrom is shifting character; a high school football star of twenty six years young boy engaged in the job of selling of kitchen gadgets. He is married to a salesgirl Janice who is pregnant but being confused and bewildered he leaves his wife and is lost in his own helpless detachment and estrangement. The post-modern writers such as John Barth, William Gaddis, Kurt Vonnegut and Bruce Jay Friedman extensively use irony, playfulness and black humor. The postmodern writers portray the modern world as a bleak, barren abyss where human civilisation faces its decline. Updike uses black humor to diminish the disgust of the nihilistic modern life. In his novel *Rabbit at Rest* Updike employs grotesque allegory of mythical happiness and success in America. Updike depicts the quest of the American middle class of 1980s for happiness through black humor.

Intertextuality

The technique of Intertextuality is very popular among the postmodern writers; the trend started with T.S. Eliot when he published his *The Waste Land* loaded with the allusions and the textual lines from various great writers including the Hindu scriptures. It can include an author's borrowing and transformation of the texts of other writers to bring intensity in the scenes and situations. An important element of postmodernism is its acknowledgment of previous literary works. Robert Coover's *Pinocchio in Venice*, for example, links Pinocchio to Thomas Mann's *Death in Venice*. Also, Umberto Eco's *The Name of the Rose* takes on the form of a detective novel and makes references to authors such as Aristotle, Arthur Conan Doyle, and Borges. John Updike borrowed heavily from Hawthorne's *The Scarlet Letter* Updike wrote *A Month of Sundays, Roger's Version* and *The Witches of Eastwick* under the influence of Hawthorne.

Pastiche

Jameson and Linda Hutcheon rejected parody and used the tool of pastiche to articulate his cosmic apocalyptic vision of American life. In his *The Cultural Turn: Selected Writings on the Postmodern* (1998) Jameson observes thus:

> I want here to sketch a few of the ways in which the new postmodernism expresses the inner truth of that newly emergent social order of late capitalism, but will have to limit the description to only two of its significant features, which I will call pastiche and schizophrenia; they will give us a chance to sense specificity of the postmodernist experience of space of time respectively. (Jameson 3)

Frederic Jameson rejects techniques employed by the modern writers and evolving his own perception of reality. The prose of Jameson has the sharpness of a surgeon's scalpel, the precision of a fine watch and focuses on the commonplace like the eye of an X-ray machine. Most of the critics of Jameson note that he is very difficult to understand because of his subtle and metaphorical prose style. Terry Eagleton (1986) considers it "unimaginable that anyone could read Jameson's magisterial, busily metaphorical sentences without profound pleasure, and indeed I must acknowledge that I take a book of his from the shelf as often in place of poetry or fiction as literary theory (Eagleton 66). Jameson defines pastiche in *The Cultural Turn* thus:

> Pastiche is blank parody, parody that has lost its sense of humor: pastiche is to parody what that curious thing, the modern practice of a kind of blank

> irony, is to what Wayne Booth call the stable and comic ironies of the eighteen century. (5)

Jameson argues that the old themes and styles of the 19th and 20 century have become outdated. In his topic "Death of the Subject' Jameson talks of various socio-political developments of the contemporary age. He is confronted with the same problem which Eliot confronted when he wrote *The Waste Land.* Eliot needed a new medium so he turned to Ezra Pound and Baudelaire for inspiration. Jameson observes that individualism and individual subjects are no more relevant. He comments thus:

> Yet today, from any number of distinct perspectives, the social theorists, the psychoanalysts, even the linguists, not to speak of those of us who work in the area of culture and cultural and formal change, are all exploring the notion that this kind of individualism and personal identity is a thing of the past; that the old individual or individualists subjects is "dead", and that one might even describe the concept of the unique individual and the theoretical basis of individualism as ideological. (Jameson 6)

Jameson rejects all stylistic techniques including parody which was popular in the 18th and 19th century. He argues that in the postmodern age pastiche is the right and suitable stylistic technique to articulate the contemporary malaise of the American people. He comments thus in *The Cultural Turn:*

> Pastiche is, like parody, the imitation of a peculiar or unique style, the wearing of a stylistic mask, speech in a dead language: but it is a neutral practice of such mimicry, without parody's ulterior motive, without that still latent feeling that there exists something normal compared with which what is being imitated is rather comic. (6)

In postmodern terminology pastiche means to combine, or "paste" together, multiple elements. For example, in most of his novels John Updike uses the tool of pastiche to effectively depict the themes of absurdity of the middle class Americans. He has "pasted" elements of previous genres and styles of literature to create a new narrative voice. For example, William S. Burroughs uses science fiction, detective fiction, Margaret Atwood uses science fiction and fairy tales; Thomas Pynchon, uses elements from detective fiction, science fiction, and war fiction. In Rabbit Run there elements of fantasy and romance; in *The Poorhouse Fair,* Updike gives a poor view of the world that technology has created. Updike gives the apocalyptic view of the future of America as the novel is set in 1984. Updike uses the elements of science and fantasy and the novels have an affinity with the anti-Utopian warnings of Orwell and Huxley. Being influenced by Albert Camus and Sartre, Updike uses absurdity and humor to portray America embracing pop culture. He creates a fictional world that creates the sentiments of the middle class Americans. Like Bakhtin, Updike uses all tools of irony, satire and burlesque the middle-class characters.

Meta-fiction

Jameson observes that the contemporary American society is very complex differing from the traditional Victorian society. The literary devices used by the traditional writers such as Ernest Hemingway and William Faulkner are obsolete. He advocated meta-fiction and the postmodern writers such as John Updike, Thomas Pynchon and Kurt Vonnegut evolved meta-fiction to articulate the contemporary complex sensibility. For example, Updike's fiction is considered as meta-fiction and his Rabbit tetralogy is epical in dimension. All the four Rabbit novels deal with the problems of four generations of people. Updike has focused on the mysterious and the uncanny reflecting a world view that is pessimistic and challenging. His novels evince mythopoeia realism. John Irving's *The World According to Garp* is a fine example of meta-fiction. Updike imitated James Joyce's *A Portrait of the Artist* when he wrote *Rabbit Run* and *Rabbit at Rest.* Linda Hutcheon in her *Poetics of Modernism: History Theory and Fiction* (1988) observes that post-structuralism and deconstruction are the main the obvious theories that contributed to the growth of post-modernism (188). Hutcheon talks about the novels of John Updike that fictionalise the actual historical events and characters. The hero of Updike's *The Poorhouse Fair* is Stephen Conner who in Cartesian sense is a linear and rational thinker with the scientific approach to an irrational world.

Magical Realism

The Chinese novelist Mo Yan, the Nobel Prize winner wrote *Big Breasts and Wide Hips* using the technique of magic realism. Salman Rushdie wrote *The Midnight's Children* presenting his hero Saleem who has supernatural powers. In the novels of John Updike there is a unique mix of brutal incidents, magic realism, the descriptions of the scenes of nature and far flung metaphors. Updike's famous and controversial novel *Terrorist* (2006) presents the protagonist Ahmad Mulloy and who may be regarded as a radicalised Muslim. The novel is an epitome of "essentialist" work of art abounds in fantasy and uncanny episodes. Updike's *Rabbit Run* touches upon all the important issue of the 21th century; there is a fruitful commentary on the AIDS epidemic; the terrorist attack on Pan Am Flight 103 over Lockerbie and American trade war. In *Rabbit at Rest* Updike depicts Harry's moral decay and spiritual lethargy of contemporary Americans.

Mastered Irony

Irony is an important tool used by the poets and the playwrights since antiquity. Mark Antony uses this tool in his famous speech in *Julius Caesar* of Shakespeare and his famous ironical stroke "Well! Brutus is an honorable man" is memorable in the history of criticism. Irony is a significant tool to expose and ridicule the evils of society and to lash at the vices such as affectation, snobbery and prudery. Morris Niedenthal (1980) in his article "Irony and the Grammar of the Gospel" observes thus: "originates in the perception of an incongruity between what is and what ought to be and it involves a conflict between pretense and reality" (142). Jameson took inspiration from Kierkegaard who propounded the postmodernist theory of "Mastered Irony." The novelists such Kurt Vonnegut, Pynchon and Vladimir Nabokov and John Updike used this important tool in depicting the ambiguities and incongruities in the life of their characters. The postmodern writers employ mastered irony, paradox and crisp wit to articulate absurdity of life. If a hero perceives an incongruity and assumes a personal responsibility for its correction, his response is certainly heroic. But unfortunately in *Rabbit Run,* Harry Angstrom doesn't recognise the role of incongruity in his life and he goes on falling deeper and deeper. Niedenthal observes thus: "it can be the exaltation of hero figures or as applied to listeners, people are implored to be courageous, to stand up and be counted, to get involved, to do their duties, to put their lives on the line, to become heroes of the faith" (Niedenthal 144). Brad Frazier in his article "Kierkegaard on the Problems of Pure Irony" observes that "it is safe to say that Kierkegaard was preoccupied with irony and its relation to the moral life. His view of irony, though was hardly static" (Frazier 417). Indeed, in his work *The Concept of Irony* he elaborated the meaning and role of "mastered Irony".

Fragmentation

Fragmentation is another important aspect of postmodern literature. The postmodern writers use this literary technique to blend various elements concerning plot, characters, themes, imagery and symbols. The factual details of the plots of a postmodern novel are fragmented and dispersed. In a postmodern novel there is a break in the sequence of events, character development and action. It is very difficult to predict what will follow the next. The purpose of fragmentation is to depict a metaphysically unfounded, chaotic universe. It can occur in language, sentence structure or grammar.

Hyperreality

The postmodernist critics such as Jameson, Jean Baudrillard and Umberto have discussed in detail the concept of hyperreality. In simple language, it is an inability of consciousness to distinguish reality from a simulation of reality in postmodern societies of America. It is a condition in which what is real and what is fiction are juxtaposed together. It is very difficult to find a distinction between where one begins and where one ends. The physical reality is mingled with virtual reality; human intelligence is blended with artificial intelligence in literature. John Updike uses this device in all the major novels as his characters are involved in the hyper-real world ignoring the physical real world. John Updike's *The Poorhouse Fair* (1958) is based on the single day of the old people's fair, when they sell their hand made goods to the people. William Peden praised Updike in his review in *New York Times Book Review* for his interest in the common life of people and for the great clarity and precision of language. Richard Gileman talked of the split between the physical desires and the spiritual longings of the protagonists. Harry and Conner struggle for significance in the harsh and oppressive world where things are changing very fast and faith is replaced by money and sex. In the first section of the novel, the cat is killed and the wall of the Poorhouse is demolished. Both events symbolise chaos and disruption in the modern America. People who crowd the fair are a race of pleasure seekers talking about holidays, illicit affairs and physical ailments. Updike dramatises the duality of body and spirit in the characters of Conner and Hook; Conner is an ambitious manager of the Poorhouse and Hook is aged and dying. The negative influences of science and technology are emphasised like Huxley.

To conclude, the postmodern writers reject the themes, style and the techniques of the modern writers and use the postmodern devices such as pastiche, magic realism, inter-textuality, and fragmentation in their works. Jameson deconstructs the Marxian ideology from the perspective of contemporary society and the forces of change and transformation of the West. Jameson is a great American cultural critic and Marxian philosopher who wrote half a dozen famous books to interpret his own Marxian thoughts from the postmodern perspective. Jameson evolved his own dialectic in his book *Valences of Dialectic* highlighting the nature of dialectical process. Dialectical system is a comprehensive, all inclusive system and Hegel and Marx are associated with totalitarian thinking. Jameson has given his own rational response to the theory of Marxian determinism. Dialectical materialism of Marx is packed with ambiguities. Jameson concludes thus: "It would therefore be profoundly undialectical to exclude this patently undialectical description of the dialectic" (15). For Jameson, the notion of a monolithic dialectic offers something like a deconstructive manifesto: "I believe that theory is to be grasped as the perpetual and impossible attempt to deify the language of thought" (9). He gave a new direction to the contemporary writers who took inspiration from him and employed the postmodern techniques in their works.

Works Cited

Baudrillard, Jean. *The Mirror of Production.* Translated by Mark Poster. Telos Press, 1975.

---. "The Order of Simulacra." Translated by Iain Hamilton Grant. *Symbolic Exchange and Death.* Sage, 1993, pp. 50-86.

---. "The Dance of the Fossils." *The Illusion of the End.* Translated by Chris Turner. Polity Press, 1994, pp. 72-77.

Bradbury, Malcolm. *The Modern American Novel.* Yale UP, 1997.

Hassan, Ihab. *The Postmodern Turn.* Ohio State UP, 1987.

Hegel, G. W. F. Hegel. *Elements of the Philosophy of Right.* Translated by H. B. Nisbet and edited by A. Wood. Cambridge UP, 1991.

---. *Lectures on Natural Right and Political Science: The First Philosophy of Right: Heidelberg, 1817-1818.* Translated by J. M. Stewart and P. C. Hodgson, edited by the Staff of the Hegel Archive, U of California P, 1995.

---. *Phenomenology of Spirit.* Translated by A. V. Miller, OUP, 1977.

Hutcheon, Linda. *A Poetics of Postmodernism.* Routledge, 1988.

---. *The Politics of Postmodernism.* Routledge, 1989.

Gilman, Richard, "The Youth of an Author." *New Republic*, vol.25, no 7. 1963, pp. 25-26.

Jameson, Frederic. *The Political Unconscious.* Cornell UP, 1981.

---. "Postmodernism--The Cultural Logic of Late Capitalism." *New Left Review*, no. 146, 1984, pp. 53-92

Lyotard, Jean-Franois, "The Unconscious History, and Phases: Notes on *The Political Unconscious.*" *New Orleans Review*, vol. 2, no. 1, 1984, pp. 73-79.

---. *The Postmodern Condition: A Report on Knowledge,* Translated by G. Bennington & B. Massum, Manchester UP, 1984.

McHale, Brian. *Postmodernist Fiction.* Routledge, 1987.

Niedenthal, Morris. "Irony and the Grammar of the Gospel." *Semantic Scholar*, 1980.

Peden, William Minor. "Ills That Plague the Human Heart". *The New York Times Book Review,* 1959.

Updike, John. *The Poorhouse Fair.* Fawcett World Library, 1964.

CHAPTER 14

Demystifying the Paradox of First and Second Generation Diaspora: An Analytic Study of *The Namesake*

Sudhir Narayan Singh and *Stuti Lal*

Introduction

The Namesake is one of the finest works of Mira Nair as a director. Taking inspiration from Lahiri's novel, she beautifully weaves the lives of Ashima, Ashok, Sonia and Gogol, using the threads of the various facets of living away from where they belong. Various elements from the book have been borrowed into the film, portraying the crisis of belongingness. Jhumpa Lahiri, in one of her interviews, mentions, "I was, without a doubt, driven by the desire for a language to call my own" This personal struggle has been transferred on screen by Ms. Nair, by keeping 40% of the dialogues in Bengali. The most noteworthy, contrast, however, is that between the first and second generation Gangulies. While Ashima, who represents the first-generation Diaspora, deeply misses her homeland, mostly at the painful time of her first delivery, Gogol, her son, is not too proud of his Indian roots. Both Gogol, and his sister are exhausted, the very moment they step in Kolkata. "I wanna go home…", says Sonia, home referring to the USA. In one scene Gogol goes on a jog from his ancestral house in Kolkata, only to be followed by a house help, can be seen as a metaphor to run away from his Indian centre. It was only after his father's demise, a loss which leaves a never fillable vacuum, yet is indispensable, that he steps into his shoes, both literally and figuratively. Towards the end of the film, he can be seen reading Nikolai Gogol, his father's favourite author, and his namesake, which parallel to the first scene in which his father does the same in a train. Yet, this driving force was not powerful enough to bring him back to his homeland. While his mother decides to divide her time between the two countries, he is happy to stick to his birth place, a desire which can be compared with Mr Bisaws' lines from V.S. Naipaul's *A House for Mr Biswas*

> "...to have lived and died as one had been born, unnecessary and unaccommodated." (5)

Mira Nair, in one of her Interviews, said, "In India, we are raised with a world view." She continued to mention how as a child she remembered the lyrics of all the songs created by *the Beatles*. Call it the post-colonial hangover, or the mere mentality which makes us believe that the grass is always greener on the other side. The latter, however, is not just a proverb as the origin of it can be found in the poetry of Ovid (c.43 b.c.–a.d. c.18): *Fertilior seges est alenis semper in agris* (The harvest is always more fruitful in another man's fields"). The glamour and glory of the west has been attracting the inhabitants of the third world countries for over several decades now, and supporting this claim, is the fact that the decades following World War II have seen a dramatic increase in the migration movements of Indians to the United States. The liberalisation of India's economy in 1991 and the opening up of U.S. immigration policies to new populations in the 1960s have been major contributors to this trend. The Indians are on average more educated, with 75% having a bachelor's degree or higher, as compared to 29% of immigrant adults overall What is termed as 'brain drain' by several school of intellectuals, can also be viewed as an individual's choice to move to a land of better opportunities and quicker growth.

Literature Review

Author	Paper Title	Theme
Dr. Binod Mishra	East is East and West is West: A Reading of Jhumpa Lahiri's *The Namesake*	The contrast between the Indian and American Culture
Srija Sanyal	Namesake of Ashimain Jhumpa Lahiri's *The Namesake*: Comparison from the Bookand the Movie	The differences and similarities between the book and movie
Dr. Sudhir Narayan Singh	'Diasporic Concerns' and Picturisation of 'Predominance of Isolation' of Indian Woman in *The Namesake*: A Film Study	Alienation and isolation of the characters in the film

Ratna Asih Setyaningrum	Representation of India as the Root of Identity in the Film Adaptation of *The Namesake*	India as the essence of *The Namesake*

The description and analysis of Indians living and struggling in a foreign land has been one of the most widely written about topics in the world of literature. Jhumpa Lahiri's *Interpretation of Maladies* (1999) and *Unaccustomed Earth* (2008), along with Salman Rushdie *Imaginary Homelands* (1991), Fatima Farheen Mirza's *A Place for Us* (2018) and V.S. Naipaul's *A House for Mr. Biswas* (1961) are some of the works in English, dealing with themes revolving around the nuances of living away from the heart and homeland.

The Universality of Generation Gap

Literature and performing arts, as reflectors of the society, have often been showcasing the clashes between individual who are one or more generations apart. In one of the biggest heart-breaking yet romantic films of 2007, *P.S. I Love You* the central character, Holly's mother is constantly seen nagging about her choice of life partner. On a similar pattern, the 2018 theatrical release *Crazy Rich Asians* introduces us with Mrs Golding, a woman who believes that she has ownership over her son's life, unintendedly makes him flee his homeland. Be it on screen, or in real life, the gap between the parents and their ward is built owing to their drastically different set of experiences that they go through. In the ever-changing socio-cultural backdrop, what is a sin today, might become the way of the world, tomorrow.

India is known to be the land of innumerable cultures. The Constitution of India is at once a fine reflection of the Indian cultural mosaic and a practical demonstration of the continuing dialogic tradition. While recognising the rich diversity it gave equal rights to all its citizens irrespective of creed, colour, region or language A child, born in Jammu, for example, would never be acquainted with the cultural nuances of Kerala, unless they are well travelled and exposed, and vice-versa. Yes, there is an inviable thread with ties all the diversities together. Keeping the peripheral traits aside, the core of all the Indian households remains the same. Yet the individuals of the family, belonging to different generations, fail to agree at many major and minor instances. However, when the upbringing of their parents and their wards have been done in countries which are poles apart, like in *The Namesake,* the definition of 'home' and 'belongingness' definitely varies a lot.

The Parallel Worlds within the Common Worlds of Ashima, Gogol, and Moushmi

In the words of Ms Lahiri, Literature is about entering other people's consciousness, Mira Niar, through her cinematic genius, manages to build a passage into the mind of her characters, helping her audience to understand why they are the way they are.

Despite living thousands of miles away, Ashok was ready to wait for weeks for an elderly person to name his son. On the contrary, Gogol. His son, soon after joining the school, was aware enough to take decision upon which name he should be called by.

> "I wandered lonely as a cloud
> That floats on high o'er vales and hills,
> When all at once I saw a crowd,
> A host, of golden daffodils"[11]

Upon being asked to recite a poem by her father, she recites the opening lines of Wordsworth "*Daffodils*" (1802). Ironically, post her wedding, her life become as lonely as the lone cloud, wandering in search of an anchor. His alienation resonates with the lines of the poem, and so does her quest. He asks Ahima what about your parent's preference?

Ashima, question him upon his 'preference'. This incident could pe marked as the first instance of how Gogol was growing up to be an individual who was quite different from his parents.

> Ashima: "I don't want to raise Gogol in this lonely country." (37)

As Ashima lies in the hospital, struggling with the length of her maternity gown, while her body prepares to birth a new life, she is reminded of the streets of Kolkata, her family, and everything that she had left behind. In that moment of pain and happiness, she wishes to be back, to the place which she had called home. She is also apprehensive of raising her first born in a country which had a culture, very distinct from hers. She could foresee America turning her son into a true American.

Ashima's worst nightmare had turned into reality. Gogol did actually become 'Nik'. Nik would use his holy *Swastick* to smoke weed, while he dances on the typical American pop music. His *daak naam* becomes his biggest enemy, and to some extent, his Indian roots, too.

Upon being asked how old he was when he moved to America, he almost tries to conceal his connections from there. Gogol, from his heart and soul, was a true American. "I don't care what they want" was his exact words in context of his parents. Gogol was not a rebel, but just an American, 'struck' in an Indian family. The alienation was a result of the disparities in the two cultures in which he belonged.

The 'Americaness' had seeped in beyond the boundries of gender, the primary example of which is Moushmi. Upon rejecting a job offer, she taunts Nik for his expectations from her which had confined her within the boundary of her house. Despite being a Bengali wife, she was nowhere close to Ashima in terms of temperament. When she found being clutched into the matrimonial ties, she doesn't shy away from committing the sin of infidelity.

The Centre

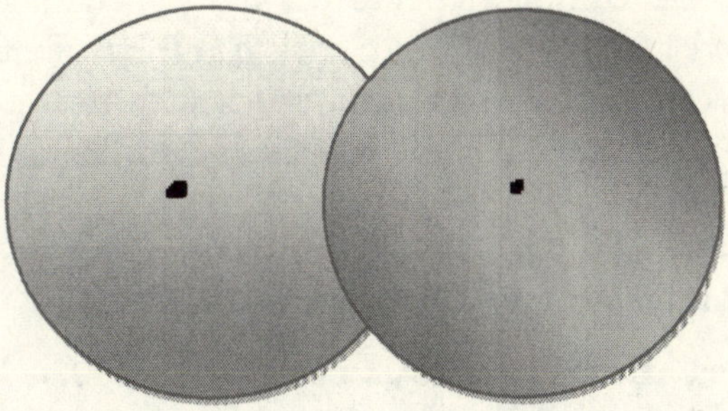

The untimely demise of Ashok proved to be a turning, especially for Gogol. All his life, especially his adult life, he had run away from his parents, living, what he thought, a perfectly carefree life. Yet post the tragedy, he curls up on his father's bed, to feel his warmth, and cries his heart out.

Gogol "I'm sorry baba." (61)

One can see drastic changes in him, drastic enough to convince the audience that he might have finally accepted his origin. While he voluntarily gets his head shaved, the visuals of his father doing the same flashes in front of his eyes. For a moment, Gogol was Ashok. The circle of life had brought them at the same place. Upon being told by his mother that he didn't has to do it, he calmly confesses that he himself wanted to.

Yet for both Ashima and Gogol, one thing didn't change. For Ashima, her centre remained in India. While Gogol, despite the life changing incident of his father's demise, couldn't shun his American centre. The longing to remain closer to the centre is beautifully projected in the last scene, where Ashima sits in Kolkata, playing Sitar, while Gogol, just like his father, reads his namesakes' novel in the train. After all their life's journey, that is where they belonged.

Indo-American vs. American in India

Cultures across the world have witnessed blurring of boundaries. For example, a lot of Christians living in India perform the *haldi* ceremony right before their wedding even though there has been no mention of the same in their holy rituals. Years of living amongst a particular culture, makes their culture, hybrid. When it comes to the diasporic children, their identity at times can be confusing to them, as showcased in a Netflix produced show called *Never Have I Ever* (2020) This comedy-drama, is all about the complicated life of a first generation Indian-American girl, named Devi. Her identity crisis, similar to that of Gogol can be explained in one line: an American, stuck with her Indian roots, however her mother, just like Ashima, was an Indian, living away from her homeland.

> "The family looked Indian but dressed as foreigners did, the children in stiff, brightly coloured clothing and caps with translucent visors." (29)

The above lines, from Lahri's *Interpretation of Maladies* (1999), confirm the urge of the second generation American to conceal their Indian identity. Where the older generation takes their Indianness as a symbol of pride, for their offspring, it is quiet the opposite. The urge to camouflage with the whites supersedes the value of their lineage.

> "Depression" was a foreign word to them, an American thing. In their opinion their children were immune from the hardships and injustices they had left behind in India..." (35)

In Lahiri's another collection of short stories, *Unaccustomed Earth,* one of the stories depicts the alienation of the naïve Indian parents, living in America, from what their American children go through, internally.

Sharing her own experience, Ms. Nair says, *"Christmas completely depresses me...I have no relationship to it, I never grew up with it."* Cloning the similar longing to belong, Mira Nair directs a beautiful scene in the film, which she describes in her own words, "*There is a Christmas tree in her [Ashima's] house, that is because she understands too early that the children growing up in America would feel alienated if one was not there.*" Going on, she talks about the heartbreakingly beautiful garage scene, *"A women, in an Indian saree, bare feet…against this conformity of suburbia with Christmas lights for me would be the light of alienation and pain…we put all her life behind her*" From her children's baby carriage, to the bikes, her entire life is behind her, yet she has nothing or none to turn to and greave. She was away from Kolkata, after all.

Generations Geneses: From Alienation to Assimilation & From Adoption to Celebration

The film, its characters and imageries, portray the classic tale of how Ashima and Ashok were complete aliens in America, and how Gogol and Sonia, assimilated with 'their' country, the same country, where their parents could never call their own. Be it having 'cool' names, or enjoying Christmas more than any other festival, their decision to assimilate cannot be deemed as a conscious choice, but just a survival tactic, which comes rather organically. On one hand their parents adapted to their American ways, by 'letting' their son live separately, or by speaking in English, throughout, while on the other hand, Gogol and Sonia celebrated their American identity by shunning all the 'baggage' that they got in inheritance from their Indian roots. Each of the individual in this beautifully made piece of art goes through their own individual journey, along with walking on the path of varied outlook towards life.

Works Cited

Doriani, Kara. *Indian Diaspora in the United States: Exploring Attitudes towards Migratory Return*. 10.13140/2.1.2052.0008. 2014.

Gramsci, A. *Intellectuals, Culture and Society*, edited by James Martin, Routledge, 2002.

Lahiri, Jhumpa. *The Namesake*. Harper Collins, 2003.

Whatley, M. & J. Batalova. *Migration Policy Institute* (Indian Immigrants in the United States. Retrieved from 2013. www.migrationinformation.org/USFocus/display.cfm?ID=962.

lithub.com/what-am-i-trying-to-leave-behind-an-interview-with-jhumpa-lahiri

sapatgramcollegeonline.co.in/attendence/classnotes/files/1589269720.pdf

www.poetryfoundation.org/poems/45521/i-wandered-lonely-as-a-cloud

www.youtube.com/watch?v=bru9oipYg18 Retrieved 26 September 2013

www.youtube.com/watch?v=2xciURpVJFg Retrieved 15 June2020

www.youtube.com/watch?v=HyOCCCbxwMQ Retrieved 16 April 2020

www.youtube.com/watch?v=tXJmT-zDbH8/te Retrieved 24 January 2008

Notes on Contributors

1. **Dr. Himanshu Parmar** is a distinguished and outstanding researcher with specialisation in Indian Literature and Romantic Poetry. During his teaching experience of around fourteen years he has authored two books titled *Across the Gaping Chasm: Social Oppression in Select Indian Novels* and *Representation of India in Select Novels.* He has also co-authored two books prescribed in the curriculum of the University. Besides, he has published many research papers in books and journals of repute. Dr. Parmar has been a resource person at many seminars and conferences and delievered keynote/valedictory addresses at numerous platforms. He is also known for his intellect and helping nature in guiding the research scholars pursuing Ph.D. under him. He is a gold-medalist in Post-Graduate Diploma in Personnel Management & Labour Welfare. To add to this, he represented Himachal Pradesh in North-Zone and National Badminton Championships and has remained a top-ranking player of Himachal Pradesh in Singles and Doubles for several years.
2. **Dr. Harpreet Kaur Vohra** is an Assistant Professor, teaches English at Panjab University Regional Centre, Ludhiana. She has a Doctorate on Margaret Atwood and has been selected for the Associate Fellowship at the Indian Institute of Advanced Study, Shimla for 2020-22. She specialises in English writing of North-East India and has published in *The Tribune, Sport in History* and the *NEHU Journal.* She has directed six plays and published a short story online.
3. **Harsimran Kaur** is a research fellow at Panjab University, Chandigarh. Her area of research includes dance studies, culture studies, Indian aesthetics, film studies and postmodernism. She is currently working on a research project in dance studies in digital era.
4. **Shubham** has been teaching English at Govt. P.G. College, Naraingarh (Ambala) for more than two years. He is simultaneously pursuing his Ph.D. from the Department of English and Cultural

Studies, Panjab University, Chandigarh. He has done his graduation and post-graduation from Hindu College, University of Delhi. His primary area of interest is Cultural Studies. He has presented papers in numerous national and international seminars/conferences. A zealous reader, Mr. Shubham has contributed a number of research papers in many edited books and research journals.

5. **Dr. Anju Jagpal** is an Associate Professor with her present posting at Govt. P.G. College, Ambala Cantt. A fellow of Indian Institute of Advanced Studies, Shimla, she is teaching undergraduate and post graduate classes for more than twenty years. She has published one book *Female Identity: A Study of Seven Indian Women Novelists*. She has published more than 10 papers in edited books and reputed national and international journals.

6. **Dr. Pooja Goyal** is an Assistant Professor with her present posting at Govt. P.G. College, Ambala Cantt. She is teaching undergraduate and post graduate classes for around ten years. She has published numerous research papers in books and reputed national and international journals. She has participated and presented papers in various national and international seminars and conferences.

7. **Dr. Maroua Rogti** is a lecturer in the department of English at Higher College of Teachers (ENS) of Laghouat, Algeria. She holds a Doctorate degree in Didactics. She is interested in the field of Didactics of English language, Psycho-Pedagogy, and teaching literacy. She is pursuing her Post-Doctorate research in the field of Educational Psychology. She has presented papers in numerous national and international seminars/conferences and has published many research papers in Algeria and abroad.

8. **Dr. Urmil Rawat** is an Associate Professor, Department of English, Govt. P.G. College, Solan. She has a teaching experience of more than 35 years. She is a well-known academician and presented her research work in various national and international seminars and conferences. Her research work has been published in numerous books and journals of national and international repute. She has guided many scholars for M.Phil. and Ph.D.

9. **Sudipta Sardar** is Vice Principal at Rabindra Bharati Mahavidyalaya, Kolaghat, Purba Medinipur, West Bengal. He has participated in several national and international seminars and conferences. He is pursuing his Ph.D. from Calcutta University. His research work

focuses colonial and post-colonial perspective on the light of history of railways and modern historical trends and historiography context.

10. **Dr. J. Iswarya** is an Assistant Professor of English in Emerald Heights College for Women, Ooty. Her research interests include Contemporary Fiction, Postmodern Literature, Contemporary Literary Theory and Contemporary Cinema. She has published her research articles in several National and International Journals and has won many awards including International-Teaching Excellence Award by ESN Publications and International Outstanding Academic Excellence Award by Green ThinkerZ Society. She is recognised for contributing to a Record Event – Maximum Authors Contributing for a Book on COVID19, registered in India Book of Records and Asia Book of Records. Currently, she teaches Literary Theory, Criticism, British Drama and American Literature to Undergraduate and Postgraduate Students and also delivers guest lectures on Contemporary Literary Theory, Postmodern Literature and other topics related to English Literature for Competitive Exams.

11. **Dr. Aditi Abhishikta** is an accomplished professional equipped with versatile knowledge and experience (22 years) in the fields of education, fine arts, classical vocal and social work, besides having a profound interest in English poetry. She is a poet, creative writer, vocalist, painter, soft skills trainer and a motivational speaker. She has to her credit more than 30 articles and poems which have been published in journals of repute; edited books and also presented papers in more than 30 National and International conferences. She has been conferred with the Best Academician Award by Elsevier SSRN Research in 2020.

12. **Anshuman** is currently a research scholar in the Department of English of Indira Gandhi University, Rewari. She qualified UGC-NET in December 2018 and did Masters in English literature in 2019 from PGGCG-11 Chandigarh. Having an online certification in Shakespeare's *Hamlet* with special reference to Ghost from Harvard University. Anshuman has won national level essay writing competition held in CRA College, Sonipat. She has presented research papers in several national and international conferences/seminars. She has published several research papers in UGC CARE listed journals.

13. **Radhika** is a research scholar in the Department of English and Foreign Languages, Central University of Haryana, Mahendergarh.

She has participated and presented a number of research papers in various national and international seminars/ conferences/ journals. Her areas of interest include Mythological Fiction, Cultural Studies and Diaspora.

14. **Upanisha S.** is a full-time research scholar in the Department of English, Avinashilingam Institute for Home Science and Higher Education for Women, Coimbatore. She is working in the field of trauma theory. She has around three years of experience in the fields of freelance spoken English training, content writing, and academic writing.
15. **Vijaykumar Ganpatrao Pawar** is an Assistant Professor & Head, Department of English at Master Deenanath Mangeshkar Mahavidyalaya, Aurad Shahajani. He is having a teaching experience of 12 years. His areas of interest are American literature and ELT.
16. **Dr. Anum Mirza** is currently working as the Women Welfare Officer (MSK), under the Ministry of Women & Child Development, Govt of India, in the district Rajouri of UT of Jammu & Kashmir. She has completed her M.A in English from University of Jammu in 2015 and Ph.D. in English from Lovely Professional University, Punjab in 2020. Her areas of interest include Cultural Studies, Trauma Narratives and Literary Theory along with Dramatic Poetry. She has also published a number of research articles in various reputed journals and books.
17. **Dr. Sudhir Narayan Singh** is a bilingual poet, editor, critic and short story writer. He started his career by teaching English to visually challenged students. He rendered services at various colleges & institutes of Uttar Pradesh, Haryana, and Punjab as English faculty and ELT-Trainer. Presently, he is working as an Associate Professor of English & Head, Humanities and Management Science Department, MMMUT, Gorakhpur, UP, India. Dr Singh acted as a resource person at HRDC-DDUGU, Gorakhpur, UP, UGC-ASC, BPSMV, Sonipat and UGC-ASC, GJUS&T, Hisar, Haryana. He has attended over 70 national/international seminars/conferences: and chaired technical sessions at IIM-Bangalore, BITS Pilani, SRM University and many other institutions of repute. He has co-authored two books *Formal Letters* and *Feminine Consciousness: Glimpsing Indian Perspectives.*
18. **Stuti Lal** is currently working as a Faculty of English at Frankfinn Institute. Apart from her love for literature, she has expertise in

English Language & Communication Teaching, Business & Corporate Training, Soft Skills & Personality Development, and Teaching English as a Second Language (ESL). A University of Lucknow alumina, Stuti believes that language is the most powerful weapon in the world, and thus wants to strengthen the global tongue of as many individuals as possible. Having headed a number of Model United Nations Conferences at institutes like IIT Kanpur, she acknowledges the value of diverse knowledge.

Index